THE SHORTEST INVESTMENT BOOK EVER

D1565427

THE SHORTEST INVESTMENT BOOK EVER

WALL STREET SECRETS FOR MAKING EVERY DOLLAR COUNT

JAMES O'DONNELL

NORTHFIELD PUBLISHING
CHICAGO

© 2008 by
JAMES O'DONNELL

Cover Design:
Interior Design: Ragont Design
Editor: Christopher Reese

Library of Congress Cataloging-in-Publication Data

O'Donnell, James, 1948-
   The shortest investment book ever : Wall Street secrets for
making every dollar count / James O'Donnell.
      p. cm.
   ISBN 978-0-8024-4652-7
   1. Retirement income—Planning. 2. Investments. 3. Saving
and investment. I. Title.
HG179.O36 2008
332.67'8--dc22

                                                          2008025381

We hope you enjoy this book from Northfield Publishing. Our goal is to provide high-quality, thought-provoking books and products that connect truth to your real needs and challenges. For more information on other books and products written and produced from a biblical perspective, go to www.moodypublishers.com or write to:

Northfield Publishing
820 N. LaSalle Boulevard
Chicago, IL 60610

1 3 5 7 9 10 8 6 4 2

Printed in the United States of America

Dedicated to millions of Americans
who need to save for their retirement

CONTENTS

INTRODUCTION
What Would You Do . . . ?

What would you do if your loved ones were heading for disaster? If, say, they were driving around with bald tires or bad brakes? Maybe missing a couple of lug nuts on their front wheels?

You'd warn them, right? Maybe help them get things fixed.

But suppose instead of thanking you for your concern, they told you, "What, me worry? I'll be fine." Or maybe, "I know what I'm doing. Thanks anyway for your kind offer."

I spent a big chunk of my adult life working for some of the best money management companies in the world, helping to make rich (and not so rich) people richer. It was good work, it paid well, and it gave me the freedom to leave the rat race early and do something else—something

I thought was more important. For me, that meant teaching at a small college in the Midwest, trying to help my students understand the ins and outs of business, money, and economics too. It's been great work. It doesn't pay as much as my earlier work did, but the opportunity to invest in the rising generation is worth more to me than another vacation or a second home at the beach.

But you know what?

It's not enough. In spite of the satisfaction I gain from helping the next generation develop economic savvy, it's not enough. I'm worried about *this* generation. Our nation is facing a financial crisis of monumental proportions. There are millions of people approaching retirement who have nothing more than some digital photos stored up in their cameras to carry them through their "Golden Years." They don't realize what it takes to retire, and they don't seem all that interested in finding help.

Yikes!

Few realize what it will be like to wake up each morning without enough to live on. Talk about bad brakes. Many of our fellow citizens imagine their retirement brimming with choices—fantasizing, maybe more like it. True enough, I do know some retired people who are living out their dreams, or devoting large blocks of time to charitable organizations, mentoring young people, investing in civic affairs, and volunteering for service overseas. Even in retirement, these people work as hard as the rest of us, and they love it. It's one of the special rewards of careful preparation.

But careful preparation for tomorrow means checking lug nuts today. It means stopping the car long enough to kick the tires and test the brakes.

Many think Social Security will be enough. That it will be a reasonable "fallback." I beg to differ. At some point in the near future counting on Social Security may be like watching for the Easter Bunny. There are better ways to spend one's time.

Like planning ahead.

There's no shortage of books or speakers on saving and retirement. But for most people, they don't work. They're like tent-meeting conversions with lots of conviction but little follow-through.

The spirit may be willing, but the flesh . . . well, it just has to have its way. And it does—"the way" of irresponsibility and reckless spending. It hurts us again and again.

So why am I adding one more book to encourage saving for later years? Well, maybe I'm just crazy, but I think we need a different kind of book. We need one that is short on jargon, charts, and mind-numbing details. We need one that helps us save where most of us save for retirement—at work, in payroll savings plans— but also covers options outside the workplace. Forget about "return characteristics," "terminal values," and "discounted future cash flow." I think we need a book that, like Detective Joe Friday of the old TV show *Dragnet*, gives us "just the facts."

Maybe, just maybe, given my own experience "in the business" and in the classroom, I can write such a book for those of us who want "just the facts" on saving for retirement.

Just the meat and potatoes, in other words.

That said, I can't make you read it carefully. Or, if you do read it carefully, I can't make you apply its principles or change your spending habits. In other words, what I can't give you—no matter how much I wish I could—is the kind of conviction that would STOP you in your tracks from spending your brains out on comforts and consumption and start you, once and for all, onto the path of saving for your fast-approaching future— AND do so with a resolve so strong that it just might save your retirement years from misery and poverty. I want to give you that kind of conviction—as if saving money could stop an advancing enemy invasion in your backyard or cure you of a disease that is ravaging your body.

Put still differently, what I used to do to make big money for wealthy people—and that I now teach my salt-of-the-earth Midwest students—that's what I want to share with you in these few, concise pages.

And all for the price of this little book.

So, as the Book of Common Prayer says, "read, mark, learn, and inwardly digest" these contents.

Your own and your family's financial future lies just ahead, around the next bend. There's no better time to examine your preparedness and to learn how to invest for a brighter and more confident future.

"HOUSTON, WE HAVE A PROBLEM"

1

(AS DOES *New York, Green Bay, and Kansas City too.)*

Remember that line?

It's from the 1995 movie *Apollo 13*, the moon mission that almost ended in outer space. The three astronauts on board Apollo 13, you may recall, had a big problem. An electrical fire ignited an oxygen tank and had blown out an entire section of their fragile ship. And with those words, "Houston, we have a problem," the astronauts called Mission Control to see if anything could be done to get them home. You probably know they made it—but only by the skin of their teeth.

Their particular resourcefulness and good fortune are not, however, going to save your own future retirement as you hurtle through space and time toward your tommorow.

So, if you've come this far, maybe you're wondering, "What can I do?"

I was hoping you'd ask.

First, stop spending so much money.

Now!

Today.

Stop threatening tomorrow by squandering what you still have today. Stop the leak in your boat.

Stopping will not, of course, be easy. Like smoking and overeating, it's hard to cut spending cold turkey. You may have even tried many times before—with no success!

But consider the potential train wreck barreling down the track:

> On average, you're going to live 20 or more years in retirement—women probably longer—whether you're prepared to live 20 years more or not . . . whether you have the money or not.

> On average, people think they will spend LESS money in retirement. "Twenty percent less" is often cited, because of, for example, lower commuting expenses and less need to buy nice work clothes. However, this assumption is more often just wishful thinking.

15

▶ On average, the more you earned during your work life, the less income—percentage-wise—Social Security will replace. And what about health care costs? Medicare, which will help, won't kick in until you reach 65. Period. And while no one in this world knows the future, the further below, say, age 45 you are today, the less certain you should be that Social Security will look and act as it does now. More likely, it will look worse.

▶ On average, count on inflation. Even "a little bit" of inflation can be like a "little" colony of termites in your basement. Can a few termites hurt that much? Well, with inflation of "only" 5% a year, your purchasing power (or savings) will be cut in half in just 12 years. Even at 3%, your money will be halved in about 20. This is not good news.

▶ On average, most of us want to help our kids (or grandkids) through college. Or we'd like to assist our elderly parents. Maybe we have charitable interests we'd like to support, not to mention crisis victims or other urgent causes around the world. "Hoping" we'll be able to do any of this is fine. But hoping is no way to fund a lifestyle of generosity, let alone a retirement lasting two decades or more.

▶ On average, back in 1950, there were 16.1 workers supporting every Social Security beneficiary. Today, they are only 3.4. And by 2040? There will be only 2.1 workers. Even conservative estimates point to the entire system running out of money in a couple of decades. (We'll look at this more closely in the next chapter.)

And speaking of running out of money, so too are many of us. Lots of us are running on empty when it comes to our own retirements. We're living paycheck to paycheck—two weeks at best from insolvency. Too many are addicted to fantasy lifestyles. We don't have enough for today, and we don't want to think about tomorrow. And as for retiring early—the dream of so many? For most of us, it's just a mirage.

These are ugly facts, my friends. But facts they are. And as adults, let alone as people who may want to help others, we need to face the facts.

THANKS ANYWAY . . .

2

I'm Covered by Social Security

SURE YOU ARE! *You, me, and millions of others. Right?*

For just a moment, let me tell you a bit more about your Social Security benefits.

As I mentioned in the previous chapter, it's hard to tell whether Social Security will be able to sustain itself in the coming decades. But certainly today, like many of us, it lives way beyond its means. It's nice to think about its being there, but there's actually not much there. And as we look to the future, it's tough to predict what the system will look like, because Social Security itself is not on good financial footing.

Let's start with how much you will get.

As I wrote earlier, the less you've earned from work during your career, the more—in percentage terms—

Social Security will replace. In rough numbers, if you earn $20,000 a year at the end of your work life, you might have about 65% of your income replaced by Social Security. That works out to about $13,000 a year, or a little over $1,000 a month.

However, if you make $100,000 a year just before you retire, you might have only about 20% of your regular income replaced by Social Security. Please understand! This is very important—Social Security benefits, per person, currently max out today under $20,000 a year. That's it. Whether your name is Rocky or Rockefeller! Whether you made $5.50 an hour during your career or $5.5 million a year! What you *used to make* doesn't really matter. Social Security is not an income replacement program; it's a safety net against abject poverty. Looked at properly you should see it as a foundation for your retirement, not the whole enchilada.

While we're on the subject, here are a few other things you might want to keep in mind about Social Security benefits:

> Unless you're disabled, your benefits won't start until you turn 62. However, if you begin taking benefits at 62, you'll forgo up to 25% of what you might have received by taking them that early.

▶ To the folks at Social Security, regardless of when you want to retire, "normal" retirement means somewhere between 65 and 67 years old, depending on when you were born. It does not mean 50 or 55. Or whenever you're fed up with work.

▶ On the other hand, if you choose to retire later—say at 68—holding off starting your Social Security benefits until then will help. By waiting, you'll be adding extra income to your monthly benefit check for the rest of your life. Better still, you may want to wait until you're 70 and get an even bigger check each month! While you don't know how long you'll live, the longer you wait to begin receiving Social Security, the bigger the check will be each month for the rest of your life.

▶ The Social Security Administration has some "breakeven" tables to help you decide how long you might live if you reach a certain age. Obviously, these tables are no guarantee of longevity, but they're handy for planning when to start claiming Social Security. For example, see:
  • http://www.ssa.gov/retire2/agereduction.htm

- http://www.ssa.gov/OACT/quickcalc/when2retire.html
- http://www.ssa.gov/planners/calculators.htm

▶ Your Social Security benefits will include health care coverage under Medicare. However, there are no Medicare benefits for retirees under 65.

▶ Here's something else not well known about Social Security and important in an age when divorce occurs almost as often as spouses get the flu. If two spouses work at least 40 "quarters" (quarters of a year, or three months), each spouse will get his and her own separate Social Security lifetime retirement benefit. However, a nonworking spouse will get half the benefit of a working spouse, if the nonworking spouse has been married to the working spouse for 10 years or more. And, after the working spouse dies, the nonworking spouse gets the full benefit the working spouse had for the rest of his or her life.

I once met with a nice woman who was exceedingly unhappy at work. Knowing I was familiar with money and retirement matters, this lady, then aged 48, asked me about early retirement. So, over a bagel, we talked. She told me she was thinking of retiring. At 48. She said she'd had enough and wanted out as soon as possible.

Clearly, she didn't expect a free lunch from Social Security, but she felt she must have, by 48, earned some Social Security benefits. She asked me how much she'd receive if she retired right now.

"Zero," I said.

She looked stunned. She didn't seem to understand how I could have calculated that so quickly. "Very simple," I said. "There are no Social Security benefits for people who retire before 62, unless they're disabled."

I wished I could have been of more help to this nice lady. Then again, at least she didn't quit her job first and find out later. Nor should you. Social Security is not likely to cause anyone to go out and celebrate. It will help, no doubt. But the less you have to depend on it, the better.

WAIT A MINUTE!—

You May Already Be Done with This Book: The Case for Lifecycle Funds

FOR SOME *reading this book, this might be the end.*

That's right! Three short chapters in, and you might already be finished.

For in this chapter you may discover all you'll ever need to know about saving for retirement. They're called "lifecycle funds" or "target-dated" funds. And what you'll discover is that, although they're not perfect, there are now mutual funds out there of this type that may be good enough. Especially if you really hate thinking about investments!

So read on. Or at least to the end of this chapter.

Back in my school days, I had a couple of friends who just tensed up whenever we had to compute stuff. I'm not thinking of friends who were stupid or lazy.

Maybe they just got scared once the teacher started to let the formulas fly. To them, it may have been like riding in a plane when the turbulence really starts rocking and rolling and the overhead bins open up and the drinks fly all over the place. Whatever it was, you just knew these folks were not likely to become, say, math professors or nuclear physicists. And while those in English class who didn't like to read could find the Cliffs Notes for most of the books we'd study, no such easy-to-follow resource was available to overcome the fright of computing quadratic equations or balancing chemistry problems. And while I no longer meet adults fretting over their algebra homework, I meet a lot of nice people who are scared to death about investing for their retirement. This can have the same kind of effect on grown-ups that formulas and equations used to have on my math-challenged friends.

And if you're one of those folks, relax, there's nothing to be ashamed of.

There will always be those who don't have the time, patience, or confidence to explore and decide on their best investment options. After all, few of us do our own dental work, right? So why do we have to get involved in investments? If OnStar can help me when I'm lost, isn't there anything out there that can save me from retirement planning anxiety?

Guess what? Now there is!

Sort of.

The "answer" is called the lifecycle (or target-dated) fund. And it's actually not half bad. (If only my old school friends could have found something this helpful.)

So even before you pour yourself that nice cup of coffee and get settled in with this engaging little investment book, we'll take a quick tour of these retirement funds that do all the work for you.

Neat, huh?

Lifecycle funds, which give you the "answers to the retirement test questions," are currently being sold by many good mutual fund companies, including many that may already be at your workplace to help you save for your retirement. Of course, I don't know what mutual funds are offered to you through your workplace plan. In this book, I'm trying to help you make good choices with whatever you have to work with. In the Appendix, I offer some specific fund suggestions for utilizing the most commonly used mutual fund companies in America. You'll also find a glossary in the back to help you understand the vocabulary of investing.

A lot of people, I promise you, would actually "get" the basics of investing, if only someone explained it in terms that the nonprofessional could understand. Also, as you read this book, write down questions that you will want to ask someone in your benefits office at work or, maybe, at the fund group your employer uses for your retirement savings plan. With this book in one hand to guide you, and answers to your specific questions in the other hand, you'll be well on your way to constructing a well-balanced retirement savings plan based on sound investment principles.

Now I just mentioned "investment principles." What I mean is that regardless of the fund group, or groups, that are available to you at work or outside of work, I want you to keep in mind some overarching principles you must remember as you invest for your retirement.

These principles include:

- Discipline (covered in chapters 1–2)
- Diversification (chapter 4)
- Low costs (chapter 4)
- Time (chapter 5)
- Consideration of circumstances beyond your control (see the daily newspaper)

Now by reading this book you can learn lots about each of these important things. And remember, I believe that many of you could, if you choose to, learn to invest on your own. Still, many people don't have the discipline or won't take the time to learn. Furthermore, some will hire "experts" (who are really salespeople) to help them. And those folks will wind up with mixed results from working with their helpers.

This is where lifecycle funds might come in. They can do for you and your investments only what needs doing and do it, hopefully, at a fair price.

Currently, lifecycle funds are available at five-year intervals for people retiring from about 2010 to 2050. All you need to do is pick the year nearest your retirement date, open an account, and fund it year after year. That's it. Whether you're a 30-year-old or a 55-year-old, you don't have to worry about the proportion of stock you should hold or how much money to keep in bonds after you turn 60. The lifecycle fund does all that for you. Automatically, too. Today, these funds may already be available to you in your employer's payroll deduction retirement savings plan.

And, afterwards, when you enter retirement, your lifecycle fund goes right on making the changes necessary in your portfolio (which is just a fancy word for your very own collection of retirement investments) to maximize the chances that you will not outlive your money.

Lifecycle funds have a set percentage of stocks and bonds in them, based on what's appropriate for someone who is either a certain number of years from retirement or already in retirement. The stock portion of the fund may or may not include both foreign and domestic issues. (They should include both; so, if a lifecycle fund is available to you, look for one that includes *both* US and foreign stocks.) The bonds, too, will have—or should have—reasonable diversification—that is, a mix of different kinds of bonds to help cut down the risks of owning too much of one thing.

To make sure I don't lose anyone early on, let me define some terms here. Stocks (or equities) are little slices of ownership in businesses, and bonds are just loans to businesses and other organizations that need money. Bonds pay interest, whereas stocks may pay dividends and tend to be more risky. But stocks also tend, over long periods, to return more than bonds. But we'll say more about returns later on.

If you're decades from retirement, your lifecycle fund will be heavily (like 70% or so) invested in stocks —domestic and foreign. On the other hand, bonds will make up a much smaller percentage (maybe 30% or less) of the fund. Then, slowly, as you keep working and contributing to your lifecycle fund, and as you get nearer retirement, the bond portion of the portfolio will gradually creep up, while the stock portion will gradually shrink. But the stock portion will—or should—continue to be an important component of the fund, right up to and into retirement and later life. It has to, if your purchasing power is to be maintained.

This shifting of assets from more stock to less stock, from fewer bonds to more bonds, as you grow older, dampens the risk of investing too much in riskier, but higher-returning stocks.

So there you are. If you'd rather not bother learning how to invest for your retirement, stop right here. Lifecycle funds are for you. They offer a good, if not "perfect," alternative for you (there are no perfect alternatives). They may also help you avoid suffering a horrendous reversal of fortunes from listening to your cousin Larry, who is convinced that stock options on a windmill farm off the coast of the Philippines is where "the smart money is going."

Now, you may be wondering, "Is there a catch?" With so much good to say about lifecycle funds, are there any drawbacks?

Well, yes. As of now, lifecycle funds don't take diversification as far as I think they should to protect and grow your portfolio. Nor do they expose you to all major equity-oriented asset classes—meaning "stock-like investments," including real estate. I'll have more to say about this later on, but suffice it to say that a prudent investor should have wide exposure to a variety of equity-oriented investments. However, to date, I have yet to see a lifecycle fund investing in real estate or taking small positions in emerging market stocks. Additionally, some mutual fund families may overload their lifecycle funds with too much of the same kind of asset, say, US company stocks.

Also, if you choose to go the way of lifecycle funds, be careful to choose a fund or funds that charge modest fees. Look to pay, if possible, no more than 0.5% per year. Even though you don't know what kinds of year-to-year returns you will get, you can still control how much you pay. So choose a lifecycle fund with low fees.

However, if you're more the hands-on type who would rather take active control of your investments and benefit from a wider range of choices . . . pour that cup of coffee and read on!

WHAT YOU SHOULD KNOW

4

about Diversification and Costs

LET'S SAY *you're not one to go with the lifecycle or target-dated funds discussed in the previous chapter.*

You'd rather call your own shots. Or try to. Good for you—an admirable choice that will serve you well.

Two of the most important issues to keep in mind when setting up your own retirement savings portfolio are *diversification* and *costs*. So pay close attention.

Let's start with diversification.

Stocks, bonds, real estate, and cash are all assets, meaning things you own that have value. Good investment portfolios "diversify" (vary or spread out) their holdings among several types of assets. Diversification is accomplished through *asset allocation*—that is, investing different percentages of your retirement money in different kinds of assets. How you allocate your assets depends on your goals, personality, and approach to risk.

Some people hold ten different stocks and think they are well diversified. Others hold three or four stock mutual funds and feel they are well diversified.

But neither is.

Anybody old enough to have invested in the early 2000s, when the market tanked, knows the benefit of a well-diversified portfolio. Let's say you were investing back then and favored three funds comprised mainly of technology or "dot–com" stocks. Well, perhaps I shouldn't bring up bad memories . . .

But the point is, NON-diversified portfolios can hold great amounts of unforeseen risk for their owners and, when things go wrong—as they will from time to time—take it real bad on the chin.

A well-diversified portfolio, on the other hand, would be one in which an investor's assets (in things such as stocks and bonds) have "return characteristics" that are not in sync with each other. In other words, when one asset zigs, another zags. Put another way, at times some assets rise while others fall. Some assets might even fall while others are going up. As long as the assets in your portfolio don't all share the same *return characteristics*, you'll be in a better place during the inevitable periods of market ups and downs.

Now remember, the assets in your retirement portfolio should not all be the same kind of asset—say, US stocks. Those of us who build portfolios for others refer to the way in which assets perform in relation to each other as their *correlation*, a concept related to the "return characteristics" of your assets. When it comes to assets in a portfolio, you don't want your assets to be highly correlated with each other—all going up or down at the same time. Low correlation makes for a good retirement portfolio.

Are you with me so far?

What you and I want for our retirement portfolios are differently performing assets, some of which climb while others dip. These kinds of offsetting movements generally dampen the risks of investing. That's the idea behind seeking low-correlating assets. But since it's hard to find assets that are *completely* uncorrelated, we at least want assets that don't correlate well. This is why you don't want a portfolio made up of only stocks. Or only bonds. Or only real estate (ouch!). Because if all you hold is real estate, you'll feel great when it's going up . . . but you'll toss in bed when the bottom falls out. (And the bottom will fall out periodically on every kind of asset.)

So what makes up a good retirement investment portfolio? A portfolio composed mainly of *equity-oriented* funds (investments that give you some share of ownership, unlike bonds). That's because investment studies, as well as history, show that, over long periods of time, the ups of equity ownership should significantly compensate you for their occasional downs.

By weaving some bonds funds (which are loans, remember) into your portfolio, you take on other kinds of assets somewhat uncorrelated to your equity-oriented assets. The combination of equity-oriented investments with bonds will likely lower your long-term investment returns only a little bit compared to a much greater reduction in the overall risk in your portfolio—a nice trade-off.

Then, if among your equity mutual funds you blend in some foreign mutual funds, along with some real estate mutual funds and emerging markets funds, you reach a nicely diversified, reasonably uncorrelated portfolio, capable of providing decent returns of, say, 8 to 10% over the life of your retirement portfolio. (And by the way, don't expect much more than this without exposing yourself to way more risk than you'll probably be comfortable with.)

Later on I'll explain how much to invest in each of the asset classes I just mentioned (US mutual funds, foreign funds, bond funds, and so on). At this point I just want to introduce you to the concept of efficient diversification.

Now let's talk about *costs* and how important they are.

Costs matter a lot. A whole lot! Since we don't know what the future will bring in terms of returns on our well-diversified portfolios (likely about 8 to 10%, remember), be careful NOT to pay too much in fees for the *funding vehicles*—that is, the mutual funds—that make up your portfolio.

If possible, you'll want to buy *low-cost, no-load, index funds*.

Low-cost means expenses associated with managing the funds in your portfolio average, ideally, no more than 0.5% per year (you can learn about fund expenses by asking someone at the fund. Or, if you can stand it, try looking them up in the fund's prospectus).

No-load means the fund is sold to you without a sales charge. If you buy your funds through a broker or through some other type of middle person—a "helper," in other words—you will be less likely able to buy low-cost or no-load funds. The thing to keep in mind, though, is that you may have a choice; you may be able to invest on your own. Nowadays it's very easy to buy funds without a broker.

An *index fund* is simply a mutual fund that tries to match the portfolio of a broad-based index, with index meaning a representative sample. Let me give you a couple of examples. Have you heard of the S&P 500 index? It's an index made up of 500 US stocks that tries to measure the performance of the entire US stock market. Similarly, the Consumer Price Index focuses on only a "basket" of items people buy, yet it tries to measure overall US inflation.

Investors who use index funds are using "passive" management, because there is no portfolio manager calling the shots as to when to buy and when to sell the holdings in the index portfolio. Holdings in an index fund change only when the composition of the index itself changes. On the other hand, "active" management, which does not typically use index funds, involves bright men and women researching new investment ideas and putting them into a mutual fund they are managing.

You might think that those bright people with their

good ideas and who make a lot of money would perform better than a passive index does. But history does not support such a conclusion. The average actively managed fund does not generally do as well as the passively managed index fund. Lots of reasons may explain why active managers don't do as well as index funds. The extra costs to actively manage a mutual fund pose significant hurdles. However, in some cases, the active folks' portfolios do work out better. (Ever heard of Warren Buffett, for instance?) Still the larger, longer record of active managers does not favor their results over passively managed index funds. So this little book recommends you use low-cost, no-load, index funds in constructing your retirement investment program.

More specifically, what you will want to do is invest in funds that follow the allocation percentages I will lay out for you in chapter 7, "More on Funds."

But let me take a minute right now to give you a clearer picture of fund expenses, something that most mutual fund companies don't want you to look into. You can do this yourself with the funds available in your own employer's 401(k) or 403(b) plan. Here, however, I'll use fund expenses for the Vanguard Group as an illustration, because Vanguard's charges are among the very lowest in the business.

If you want 40% of your investments in US stocks, the Vanguard Total Stock Index Fund costs 0.15% per year. That's fifteen one-hundredths of one percent a year. About $1.50 a year per $1,000 you invest. Now, that's low! Very low! You can find fees even lower out there, but across the entire investment spectrum, Vanguard's fees are among the very lowest. Their pricing gives you an idea of what a firm interested in their investors' welfare charges mutual fund clients who set up portfolios on their own. I want you to understand what "low costs" means, because the average, annual, management fee charged in 2008 by US stock mutual funds to oversee your investments is about 1.35% per year— or $13.50 for every $1,000 you have under management in your portfolio. And these management fees don't include loads—those sales charges that compensate your broker or advisor, if you have one.

Fees really matter over time. High fees gnaw away at your returns.

Again, I don't know what funds or fund family your employer uses with your retirement saving plan. But, unless your employer picks a high-fee provider, you don't need to and should not pay high fees. Same goes if you invest on your own. But even if you are willing to pay high fees, the evidence does not support you're getting much for having done so. True, somebody may hold your hand; maybe take you to lunch. But high fees still don't guarantee you better investment returns.

So then, why do some people pay high fees? I'm not exactly sure. I guess some just don't know about these sorts of things. Others find a "convenience" factor or a "friendship" factor. And, for sure, lots of people just hate, or are scared of, making investment decisions and hope someone else will do better.

As for me, I just wouldn't pay higher fees than those I pay a firm like Vanguard. And since higher fees don't guarantee better returns, at least with lower fees I can control what I pay.

And I try to control that mercilessly!

THE IMPORTANCE OF TIME

5

TIME IS *your friend when you're investing your money.*

Or at least it can be if, like a good friend, you take time to understand it.

Choices that might seem foolish if, say, you need your money tomorrow, become practical —even advisable—if you won't be needing your money for a decade or more.

The focus of this book is on retirement investing, not on saving for next month's rent. Next month's rent should be kept in your checking account. But checking accounts are nonsense if you're saving for retirement many years down the road.

Here's the key point to remember about time and saving for your retirement: **if you're saving money to**

be used many years from now, time gives you the luxury—even the necessity—to take risks. In fact, if you don't take risks with long-term money, you're probably short-changing the value of your future nest egg.

Does this sound crazy? Let me give you some longer-term perspective on the power of time.

Since stocks—and other equity-oriented investments—are the best long-term generators of performance and should be at the heart of your retirement savings program, let's look at their returns over time. If we go back as far as 1900, we will find years when stocks returned as much as 54% and years when they fell as much as 43%. (By the way, stocks tend to rise about twice as often as they fall.) Those ups and downs are called volatility, and volatility is inherent in investing, as are both the thrills and anxieties it produces.

Because of their unavoidable volatility, stocks make very poor choices for investing money needed for this month's rent or next year's foot surgery. So it's better not to use stocks—or any other equity-oriented investment, for that matter—as a parking lot for money you will need in the near future. Why? Again, because at any given moment your equity-oriented investments could be worth a whole lot less than the amount you initially invested.

That being said, over longer periods of time things look very different. The longer the time period we look at, the more predictable results become. As I've already mentioned, since 1900, US stocks, as measured by the Dow Jones Industrial Average, have gone up as much as 54% and down as much as 43% in a single year. But if we stretch out the holding period of your investments, the volatility decreases.

How much?

Let's look at time periods like those over which we would save for our retirements. Let's start with 5-year holding periods. What happens? Well, over ANY 5-year period going back to 1900 (meaning 1900 to 1904, 1901 to 1905, 1943 to 1947, and so forth), stocks have risen as much as about 20% per year, and yet, in their worst 5-year period, have fallen only about 5% per year.

If we consider even longer time periods, stock returns get even tamer.

Over any 10-year stretch (which means 1900 to 1909, 1951 to 1960, etc.), the best 10-year stretch averaged close to 20% per year, while the worst such 10-year period (which, by the way, we are living through as I am writing this) has had a return of just about 0% per year for 10 years.

So, our returns from early 1999 to early 2008—10 full years—have averaged 0% a year. But then, don't forget that we never had a decade (or two, for that matter) like the 1980s and 1990s in which we got returns from stock, from 1982 to 1999, that averaged 19.85% per year.

Wow! Spectacular! And now, somewhat understandably, we're in the middle of some payback. Even in the decade of the Great Depression (1930 to 1939) we managed to eke out +0.1% per year. But in this decade of the 00s, we may not get even that—which makes the future more, not less, promising than ever.

Look at returns from stocks in another way. Even if an investor, on paper, lost a lot of money in a single year by investing in stocks, over any 10-year period, stocks almost always made some money. Maybe not lots, but some. And even if in very bad times investors got pounded by losses of as much as 54% during a single year, those poundings are effectively lessened and finally eliminated the longer the investor stays invested, which, when we think about retirement savings, is a long time.

But do you also see why you don't want the next month's rent money in stocks? Because the volatility is more unpredictable and dangerous the shorter the investor's time frame.

The longer you look at it, the better things look. If we consider 20-year periods (say, 1950 to 1969, 1961 to 1980, and so forth), the volatility gets even milder. The best 20-year returns have been as good as about 18% per year; the worst still returned about 6% a year.

And then, perhaps not surprisingly, during any 25-year period (say, from 1950 to 1974, 1951 to 1975, etc.), the best up periods and the worst down periods all converge at about 10% per year, whatever 25-year period you pick.

So remember: Over short periods of time, equity-oriented assets are like turning your home over to a hundred puppies not yet house broken and predictably wild. NOT the place to put your money. Too much risk, too much "variability of returns."

But over longer periods of time—the kind of time you have when saving for retirement—10% returns on your money begin to seem reasonable, in spite of the unpredictability of any single year's return.

Now, am I able to tell you that, year after year, you will definitely get 10% returns from that stock fund in your retirement plan? Unfortunately not. But the past at least points to a trend that may well continue. Besides, what else could you invest in that would give you a better likelihood of as good a return for your future?

And by the way, if you have an eccentric uncle who says this is all nonsense because he knows of a "sure thing" returning 25% a year without risk, thank him, offer him a donut, and hide your checkbook.

"10, 5, 3,"
and Other Rules of Thumb

6

10, 5, 3.

Remember those numbers—10, 5, 3.

Every investment book has the inevitable section about what you should invest in and how much to expect from your investments.

10, 5, 3. That's all you need to know. Maybe you hoped for more. Sorry. It's as simple as that.

Over long periods of time—without any guarantees, of course—you are likely to get a 10% return from your equity-oriented investments, 5% from bonds, and 3% from your cash. Now, those numbers don't account for inflation, taxes, or fees, but you can't control inflation or taxes, and we've already addressed fees in chapter 4 (hint: avoid them as much as possible).

Investments returning an average of 10% per year double over about seven years. If you hear someone tell you that they can get you 15 or 20% per year, especially if you're also told "there's no risk," trust me, the person telling you such nonsense is exceptionally misguided.

10, 5, 3—got it? You don't need charts and graphs and miles of words that equivocate and hem and haw over what you're likely to get. Because no one knows what you will get. We can't see into the future. If our economy and world events go well, our retirement portfolios could become very happy. But if events go poorly—say, we experience another terrorist attack—our portfolios could plunge once again.

No one knows what's ahead.

So just remember, in spite of depressions, wars, recessions, presidential elections, and assassinations, over the long term the numbers are still 10, 5, and 3.

They're probably our best guesses for the future.

Over long periods of time, and, for sure, with some anxious "bumps in the road" along the way, equity-oriented investments tend to do the best. Bonds also have their ups and downs, but they tend not to bump up quite as far—or down quite as much—as stocks. Cash—well, cash is cash. It's dull and boring. But it's safe, especially in rough times and *most especially* if you need the

47

money soon. Like tomorrow, for instance. Or next month.

Cash is also helpful, if taking risks with your money keeps you awake at night.

Now, as another rule of thumb, it's my considered opinion that most people's workplaces offer *too many*—not too few—options for retirement investment. There are, of course, stock, bond, and cash fund options in most plans, along with, in many cases, an annuity offering (which we'll get to later). That's all there should be. But most plans don't stop there. They also include other flavors and colors to choose from. You'll have a stock fund, yes. But maybe you'll also have a small-cap stock fund and a mid-cap stock fund as well. Maybe you've got a technology fund or a natural resources fund too. And the bond portion of your plan may have a "high-yield" offering as well as a Treasury fund. All these choices make retirement saving more complicated for the unsophisticated investor.

What do you do with all this stuff?

My job is to try to keep things simple for you.

Keep this in mind for the mutual funds you choose:

> ▶ Think equity-oriented funds—that is, funds that invest in stock or some kind of ownership claim on businesses or real estate.

▶ Think bonds—in which you lend your money out
and hope to get it back with interest.

▶ Think cash—things like CDs, a money market fund,
or a savings account.

Again, the retirement plan you have at work probably has nothing so simple as just three mutual funds,
one with stocks, one in bonds, and one in cash. Rather,
you probably have much more. Too many choices can
make a person feel unable or unwilling to make an investment decision at all. The more options investors
have, especially inexperienced investors, the more likely
they will delay making a decision or not join their employer's plan at all. Or maybe they'll just settle for the
lowest-risk option—the money market fund or the
annuity—which may not be the best option for the long
term. Still others may feel they can't make the right decision without spending money getting professional
help.

For those who stay out of their company's plan altogether, thankfully new laws are making that option
harder. Good thing, too! (See Chapter 12 on "free money.")

But even if your employer's retirement savings plan
has too many options, invest anyway. Learn what to do
by reading this book. Don't hurt yourself by ignoring

your employer's plan. And once you join, don't make crazy bets, like thinking you can jump in and out of the stock market at the right time. Or like thinking—by listening to your friends or television commentators—that you'll know when a market has "bottomed" or when it's due "for a correction."

Nope. Nobody knows that. But there's still much you *can* know, so read on.

As we'll discuss more in chapter 12, most employers will give you free money by matching some part, or all, of the money you contribute. (A buddy of mine gets one dollar for every two he invests. Pretty neat. Who wouldn't participate in that plan? But you'd be surprised . . .) In most cases you'll have to contribute money to your own account first, but so what? It's in your best interest to take part in your employer's retirement plan.

So where should you start?

Begin by choosing the US stock fund with the lowest costs and the widest variety of only US stocks. If you're a beginner, stay away from "hot" funds—meaning the ones that were up the most last year. Also, if your plan has them, stay away from any narrowly specialized funds. For instance, steer clear of any funds that have words in them like "small-cap" or "high-tech" or, maybe, "Croatian." Those funds are not for beginners.

They *may* not even be appropriate for more sophisticated investors. Frankly, many investment sophisticates only hurt themselves trying to get too cute.

I'll discuss how much money to put in each fund in the next chapter, but for now just try to pick out the right funds. Ideally, we're looking for four different kinds of equity-oriented funds—US stock, international stock, emerging markets stock, and real estate—and two kinds of bond funds—US Treasuries and US Treasury Inflation-Protected Securities.

Why these particular funds?

The four stock funds are the engines of your portfolio's growth, but their returns, we hope, will not be so highly correlated as to rise or fall all at the same time. The emerging markets fund should produce higher returns with higher volatility, because it captures investment activity in younger economies that are growing faster but are more volatile. The two bond funds will tend to be safer but should not be expected to grow rapidly. They are meant as shock absorbers for your portfolio. Both the Treasury Inflation-Protected fund and the real estate fund also provide protection to your portfolio in the event inflation picks up, an event which would likely do damage to the Treasury bond fund and your other equity funds.

You see, you've got to try to prepare for everything.

So let's get started with finding the funds for you. If you don't have these exact funds, try to pick funds from your company plan that get as close as possible to what I'm asking you to do. The Appendix contains a list of these funds from major investment companies.

Start by finding a fund that covers the *entire* landscape of the US stock market, not one that concentrates on a narrow niche. If your plan offers a US stock market <u>index</u> fund, grab it. Especially if it says something like "S&P 500" or "Total Stock Market." And because it is an "index," the fund should cost you very little and will have its own built-in diversification (as we discussed in chapter 4), which is a beautiful thing.

Once you've found your US stock mutual fund, next find a US Treasury bond mutual fund, if you can. Then, if there is one, find a Treasury Inflation-Protected Securities (or "TIPS") fund. And while you're at it, locate a foreign stock fund. (Foreign stock mutual funds usually come in two flavors—*international* and *global*. International funds do <u>not</u> tend to hold US stocks, while global funds can and, frequently, do. You don't want to double up on your US investments, so stick with an <u>international</u> stock mutual fund.)

Next, if you can—that is, if these are available to

you in your retirement plan—find an emerging markets stock fund and also a real estate fund (in other words, a mutual fund that invests in real estate). Wherever possible, choose funds with the lowest expenses, and, remember, look particularly for "index" mutual funds. Again, for now, we're just trying to select the right items from the menu. In the next chapter, I'll get more specific with what percentage of your assets to put in each of these funds.

If you're with me so far, you might be asking, "If stocks—or equity-oriented investments—do best in the long run, why not put everything you've got for retirement in equity-oriented mutual funds?" That is a good question based on what I told you in chapter 5 about equity-oriented returns over long periods of time. But don't forget what I told you about *correlation* back in chapter 4. If you do what I'm telling you in this book, most of your investments will wind up in stock—in equity-oriented mutual funds—just as they should. And if you're young enough, yes, you might put all of your retirement money in stock funds. But I still wouldn't recommend that, even for my youngest investors. Believe me, it's just safer—and doesn't hurt your likely returns very much—to spread your money over funds that invest in US stocks, international stocks, real estate, emerging markets stocks, AND bond mutual funds. Remember, you don't want to hold things that move up and down at the same time, to the same degree.

But one thing I want you to avoid in your retirement plan is using the very, very safest option—like cash or money market funds—as investments. They're just not a good option for long-term investing. Same goes for trying to switch into or back and forth to cash when you think the market is doing poorly or going nuts. Don't do that. Nor do I personally think you should use annuities, which are insurance contracts that give you "guaranteed" monthly income in retirement, and which are very likely among the options your employer's retirement plan offers. I'll say more about annuities in chapter 14.

Another rule of thumb (like the 10-5-3 rule) worth considering is the "125-less-your-age" rule to make a quick-and-dirty estimate as to how much to put in everything other than the bond fund. In other words, if you're 20 years old, put about 100% of your retirement money in your equity-oriented funds (because 125 less your age equals 105, which is more than 100%). So under this rule, if you're 20 years old, you might put nothing in the bond fund. (But, again, I think it would be smarter to diversify and put something in it anyway.)

On the other hand, if you're 50, you might want to have 75% in your equity funds (125 less 50 equals 75%) and 25% in your bond funds. And so on and so forth. Now, there's nothing magical about the number 125. It's just a rule of thumb to help you control some investment risk as you get older. It forces you to move toward a more balanced portfolio as you approach retirement. And while for some I may sound like I have Alzheimer's when I repeat some things, just remember that bonds tend to be less volatile than stocks. They also tend to throw off more income, and they are nicely uncorrelated with the returns you're likely to get from your equity-oriented investments. All these things serve to make bonds more welcome members of an older investor's portfolio. Bonds tend to dampen risks from owning too much equity.

Some people, very uncomfortable taking risks, may use the still more conservative "100-less-your-age" rule instead of the "125-less-your-age" rule. Under the "100-less-your-age" rule, following similar guidelines as the 125 rule, 20-year-olds would put 80% of their retirement money in equity-oriented mutual funds and 20% in bond funds. Similarly, if you're 50, you'd put 50% of your retirement funds in equity-oriented funds and 50% in bond funds. All other ages would follow the same sort of rules.

Rules of thumb (like 10-5-3, and the 125 rule) have their place, as long as they aren't followed slavishly. Whether you use the 125 or 100 rule—or even invent your own 115.5 rule—I want you to understand that using different kinds of funds (US stocks, bonds, and so forth) will help you get a good share of the investment returns available to you from the equity market (remember, that's about 10% a year, on average) and still control risk, both of which are very good things to shoot for.

In the end, you should choose investments you can live with and that let you sleep at night . . . as long as they include an equity-oriented portfolio of mutual funds throughout most of your life.

You just may want less equity the older you get.

MORE ON FUNDS

7

WHEN WE *left off last, we were having a nice little chat about equity-oriented and bond funds.*

I also made several comments about avoiding cash funds (money market funds, for instance) in your retirement account.

In this chapter, I'd like to say more about the funds you should use.

You'll need equity-oriented funds in your portfolio for as long as you live, because, regardless of your age, they are your investments' engines of growth. The only thing that will change as you grow older is the percentage of your retirement money you may want to keep in these funds. The older you get, the less you may want to keep in equity, because, as we said in the last chapter, with age you may want to dampen your investment risk a bit more. On the other hand, if you're quite young, you might want to put more of your payroll contributions into equity-oriented funds.

But remember—not everything should go into your equity-oriented funds, even though those funds will provide the bulk of your long-term returns.

As you look over the array of investment alternatives you have available from your employer's retirement plan, I want you to think about some other very important things. In the last chapter, I suggested you begin constructing your retirement portfolio with a no-load, low-cost US Stock mutual fund, preferably an index fund. Now, in that fund, you'll put about 30–35% of your total, retirement investments.

Next, let's look at your international stock fund. But before we do, let me just mention that, if you have other assets—stocks, bonds, or real estate, for instance —NOT part of your retirement plan, you may want to take into account their total value as you ponder the overall percentage allocations I am recommending in this chapter. For example, if you own a home worth, say, $100,000, you might want to consider that asset as a part of your real estate allocation before you invest more in a real estate mutual fund. The same would go for your US stock allocation, for example, if you already hold some stock in American businesses outside your retirement portfolio.

Now let me get back to the percentage allocations you should hold in your retirement portfolio.

For a long time, the good old U. S. of A. was the engine of growth that drove the entire world economy. Well, the United States is still the biggest economy in the world, but these days it's getting some help—and competition—from many other nations. Europe, for instance, has in the last decade gone from being a collection of competing nations to a union of nations that challenges the United States economy effectively around the world. And the same goes for Japan, which is today the second largest economy on earth. Europe and Japan are both examples of "developed" economies, and you should invest in "developed markets" through an international stock fund.

Also, some nations that, not long ago, were called "less-developed" are now powering up their economies in very big ways. Some of these countries used to get foreign aid from us. Some, once upon a time, were our "enemies" (Vietnam comes to mind, for example). Today, some less-developed nations are growing a lot faster than developed nations, including the USA. So if your retirement plan makes an emerging markets fund available to you, it could make good sense for your long-term retirement portfolio to put some money there, in addition to the international stock fund your plan has.

You see, there are two parts to your international investment allocation—the "developed" part of the world (Europe and Japan, for instance) and the less-developed, or "emerging markets" part. Let's look a bit more at the developed part first.

Look over the investment options available to you in your employer's retirement plan and see if you have a fund that says something like "Global Stock" or "Foreign Stock" or "International Stock." Again, if those words appear with the words "index fund," all the better. But they may not. Stay away from any fund that gives you too narrow an investment in world markets. In other words, don't use any single-country or single-industry fund, even if it's an index—things like a "Russia Fund" or the "Transylvanian Cancer Research Fund." They're way too narrow.

What you want to do, depending on your comfort with risk, of course, is to put about 25% of your total retirement assets (or 25% of all your assets, if you're counting those outside your retirement plan, too) in a foreign <u>developed countries</u>' stock fund. Ideally, you want one that says "international" (not "global"). "International," remember, means the fund invests all over the world <u>except</u> the USA (you've got that already in your US stock fund). "Global" funds can invest in the USA, as well as elsewhere. So choose an "international" fund, if you can, and choose one with low costs and lots of diversification.

Now, let's look at investing in the less-developed world. Not every employer's plan will have an "emerging markets" stock index fund, but if one is available, go for it. That's the place where the stocks of companies in those faster-growing, up-and-coming countries hang out. There's more risk in this kind of fund, but remember, risk is good when you're saving for long-term retirement. Again, it would be best if the emerging markets fund were an index fund with low costs and no loads. But whether it is or isn't, don't put too much money in. Any more than 5% of your total retirement money in emerging markets would be, in my opinion, too risky.

Next, put about 15% of your retirement funds into a low cost, no-load, real estate fund. But here you have to be very careful of expenses. Real estate funds tend to charge some hefty fees at least—more than the average stock mutual fund. TIAA-CREF and Vanguard both have high-quality, low-cost options. Many other fund groups have real estate funds but not with low-costs. Remember, wherever possible, you want to avoid high fees.

So far, we're got about 75 to 80% of your retirement money invested. It's all in equity-oriented stuff. Let's review:

US Stock	30–35%
Foreign Developed Stock	25%
Foreign Emerging Markets Stock	5%
Real Estate	15%

As for the bond portion of your retirement portfolio, keep it simple. Stick with two different US Treasury funds, if possible, for about 20 to 25% of your retirement assets. That is, invest your bond money only in investments backed by the United States Government, carrying the guarantee of the U. S. Treasury in the unlikely event of a financial holocaust. Those kinds of mutual funds will say "Treasury" somewhere in their name.

Bonds are funny beasts. Bond funds will, like stock funds, have good years (which is a wonderful fact!). But bonds are not the engines of growth for a long-term retirement portfolio. Rather, you invest in bonds because their returns are, for the most part, not particularly well correlated with your equity-oriented funds' returns. Bonds are likely to rise when stocks fall and fall when stocks rise. Since stocks rise about twice as often as they fall, and rise, on average, more than bonds, your retirement portfolios' engines of growth will likely be stocks, not bonds. But bonds can and do help offset the volatility of your other equity-oriented assets. And in those occasional years when stocks get trounced—and there will be such years—you'll be glad you held some Treasuries. They can provide that proverbial cup of cold water to a parched soul. And that parched soul could well be yours.

Now, if you invest about 20 to 25% (and maybe more as you get older) of your entire retirement portfolio in Treasury mutual funds, try to hold two different types of Treasury funds, putting about half in each. One Treasury fund should be "inflation-protected" (and say so on its wrapper), if such a fund is available in your plan. The other US Treasury fund should be a general Treasury fund that may have a combination of short, intermediate, and long-term US Treasury issues.

If your plan doesn't have a US Treasury fund—and some won't—maybe it has a high-quality US corporate bond fund with low expenses. This type of fund is somewhat more risky than a pure US Treasury fund, but you could put your bond money there if that's what you have to work with. Or, just maybe, you might invest in a Treasury fund outside your employer's plan, where—hopefully—you might have an IRA (more on that in chapter 13) in which you could do your bond investing.

As always, be careful with the total expenses you pay directly or indirectly to the mutual funds you invest in. (The true costs may be buried deep in your funds' prospectus.) Fees on bonds should be substantially lower than the expenses in your stock funds (which shouldn't be very high, either). One-half of one percent *or less* (hopefully, much less) on bond funds is both desirable and possible. As an example, know that Vanguard charges 0.2% per year for its Treasury Inflation-Protected Securities fund.

So, to review, stay away from anything exotic or anything too narrow. Stick with the fund types and asset allocations I recommend—that is, US stock (30–35%), international stock (25%), emerging markets stock (but NOT emerging market bond funds) (5%), and real estate (15%).

And put 20–25% in Treasuries: 10 or 12% in general Treasuries and about the same percentage in Inflation-Protected Treasuries.

Now you're on your way!

ARE YOU GETTING OUT OF KILTER?

8

The Need to Rebalance

OK. *Now that you've made the decision to save for retirement, found the discipline to follow through, picked the appropriate funds, and set up the right asset allocation, you're home free, right?*

Not quite.

Beyond our best thinking, discipline, and execution of our plan, lots of uncertainty about the future will continue to hang around. This book is not meant—even if you read and follow it diligently—to be an ironclad guarantee of a luxurious future in which you waltz from victory to victory, wallowing in dough. Rather, it is a carefully thought-out, long-term program, based on extensive investment experience and wide financial knowledge of what works—and what doesn't—in saving for retirement. It is best understood as a neat tool to help you do your best with what you have to work with.

Yet, the fact remains that we don't know what lies ahead.

Still, let's do what we can.

One aspect of saving for retirement that is foreseeable, and we can do something about, is the certainty that our investments will, over time, get out of whack with respect to each other. In fact, over time, they'll get out of whack again and again. The asset allocation that I recommended in the last chapter—30–35% US stocks, 25% international developed countries' stock, 15% real estate, 20–25% US Treasuries, and 5% emerging markets stock—will, with time, wander away from those percentages.

"Wander away?" What do I mean?

Say, for example, that US stocks rise and Treasuries fall. Over time, the value of your US stock allocation will rise above 35% and the value of your Treasuries will fall below 20%.

Follow what I'm driving at?

This unavoidable drift is natural, but not a good thing and must be corrected regularly. The correction process involves *rebalancing*, and this is a very good— and necessary—thing.

Don't look at this as an irresolvable problem or something that's your fault. It's just the natural, ongoing result of market dynamics.

What you will need to do, regularly and reasonably, is, within your retirement fund, exchange assets OUT OF funds that rise above your target asset allocation for that asset class and exchange assets INTO funds that fall in value below their target allocation.

This sounds simple. But, psychologically and emotionally, it can be very hard.

Think about it. What I'm asking you to do is sell some of your winners and buy more of your losers. Or at least, I'm asking you to buy more of your poorer-performing investments. And that is not easy for anybody to do. Emotionally, when you rebalance, you may feel like a nut. After all, aren't you trying to increase the long-term value of your portfolio? Why sell winners? Why not let them run—and sell the losers?

Because on Wall Street we learn: "Trees don't grow to the sky." And, "Bulls make money, and bears make money. Only pigs get slaughtered."

Follow what those old saws mean?

The more your winners are allowed to rise in price and run away from their intended percentage allocation, the more risk your portfolio takes on. And too much risk

67

is not good for you or your retirement savings. Without rebalancing regularly, your portfolio becomes overly concentrated in funds that may be getting too "hot." And back in chapters 6 and 7, you learned about the virtues of effective diversification, while in chapters 10 and 11 you will learn about the dangers of "hot" funds.

No doubt, the fund you sell out of may continue to rise for a time. And the poorer-performing fund you're now buying may continue to drift lower. Sorry. Neither you nor I can foresee the future. No one knows when the bell will ring, ending outstanding performance for one asset class and announcing rotation to another. We can only make the best choices we can based on the information we have. And if your good funds continue to rise, well, sell more of them and put the proceeds into the funds that are underperforming. What I want for you are reasonable returns with the least amount of risk. Too many investors understand only the first part of that statement. They want high returns, yes. But they ignore—with a great chance of loss—the *risk* side of investing. On the other hand, others see only risk in investing and so forgo investing altogether, choosing to plunk down their money in a CD or a savings account and leave it there.

Both approaches hurt you.

This is where rebalancing comes in and sits at the heart of good risk management. And all good money managers have to be good risk managers too.

How often should you rebalance? At least once a year. Your retirement fund at work is tax sheltered, so rebalancing doesn't produce taxable gains. On the other hand, don't drive yourself crazy with rebalancing. It is not something you'll need to do nightly or weekly. There may be long periods of time when no asset class you own gets more than 1 or 2 percentage points out of whack from its intended allocation percentage.

But at least once a year, look over the current allocations of your retirement fund assets and see if you need to make adjustments to get the allocations back in line. You don't need to rebalance if the percentages are off just a little bit. But make certain you rebalance if any asset's allocation wanders more than five percentage points out of balance.

And be tough! Because when you need to rebalance, remember, it may not be easy.

HELLO?

9

Is There Anybody Around Here Who Can Help Me?

SO, YOU'VE READ *this far—it's like climbing a mountain, isn't it?—and now you're asking yourself, "Can I really do this stuff on my own?"*

You betcha!

At least, I think you can. (But don't forget you can go back to chapter 3 anytime you want and reconsider the lifecycle fund.) Clearly, however, there are some people who, like a lot of kids in high school algebra, insist they're "just no good at math." And whether it's math or money management, they're convinced, "I JUST CAN'T DO THIS!" no matter how much they try.

But, really, if you stop to think about it, retirement investment planning is not so much like doing math or nuclear physics as it is about having a little confidence in your ability to read a little, follow directions, and maintain some discipline.

You can do that, can't you?

Easy for me to ask. Still, not everyone is comfortable swimming in these waters, no matter how simple I try to make the steps. So if you're one of those who feels uncomfortable investing on your own—including going the lifecycle route, because you still have to make certain choices—then you may need to hire someone to help you.

But if you do, PLEASE be very careful.

And have your eyes wide open.

Very wide open! Because hiring somebody and paying them to do this kind of work for you may give you the <u>illusion</u> that, if only you pay someone, you'll get the "answers to the test." Put another way, you may think you're getting someone who knows what the future holds and how you should invest to take advantage of what's up ahead.

But make no mistake about it, the fact that you're paying someone to help you gives you no guarantee that you will get good results. And while many "helpers" are honest people and may sincerely want to do the right thing, the money business attracts some people who are out there looking to take advantage of you. However, I'm much less worried about the dishonest few than I am about the many enthusiastic amateurs who don't give you much at all for what you pay. In other words, I'm concerned that you'll pay some well-meaning helper/ broker too much and get too little.

Really, the investment business isn't full of schemers, crooks, and opportunists. I think most people working in "the business" mean well. But very few have much knowledge of the inner workings of finance and investments. Most brokers/advisers and other helpers are really sales people gathering assets to make a living and servicing customers for their employers—investment houses—that have their own profit goals, which are not necessarily aligned with yours.

Here's how it usually works if you look for help in managing your money. First, you'll probably wind up with a broker, even if they refer to themselves as an "investment representative" or an "investment consultant." You might, on the other hand, find yourself with a money manager (whom I'll discuss below) or a "fee-only" financial planner (who might be quite expensive, by the way, but could be more helpful and less biased).

Brokers may also be called "advisors" or "customer service representatives" or "registered reps." They go by lots of names, in fact. But whatever they call themselves, they don't work for free.

They must be licensed. And as brokers, they usually make their money on "commissionable" sales. In other words, the investments they sell you pay them a sales commission, or a *load*, if you buy mutual funds. And if your business stays with your broker for more than a year, they probably make a smaller "trailer" commission every year your business sticks with them, which gives your broker an incentive to keep in touch.

In the past, brokers didn't get paid based on how your portfolio did, just on how much they sold you or the trading you did. But brokers and the companies that employ them are getting more clever. They are figuring out ways to make money even if you don't trade stocks or funds with them. Today, many get paid for "overseeing" your portfolio, for providing you with "peace of mind." For this service, they may charge an annual "wrap" fee—equal to maybe 1 or 2% of everything you have with the broker—just to help you manage your money.

On the other hand, money managers, should you hire one—and if you have enough money to make their services worthwhile—are paid differently. They're licensed and registered with the Securities and Exchange

Commission (the SEC). This is the side of the business I come from, by the way, not the brokerage side. Money managers don't earn commissions; they get annual "management fees" based on the total dollars they manage for you. A typical manager charges 1% (or more) on the initial amount of money you invest with them. They may have a minimum fee, in fact, to discourage small investors, who usually are of no interest to them. This usually keeps away the "little" client without the manager having to refuse his or her business. For instance, the money manager might say, "We'll take on your $400,000 account. But we'll have to charge you 1% based on our minimum account size of $500,000." So, the "little guy" winds up paying $5000 a year, if he or she comes aboard, to manage that $400,000 account, which works out to be, not 1%, but 1.25% a year in management fees. If someone cared to give the money manager $100,000—oh, the manager might take it. But the poor client would then be paying 5% a year—a prohibitive fee!—to have their account managed.

Generally, money managers have more training, education, and experience than a broker has in the management of money, and not just in "gathering customer assets." But by paying a fee, there are still no guarantees that you'll get good results.

Since money is so centrally important to so many people, and so many of us are so afraid to manage our own money, the brokerage and money management businesses will probably always have customers willing to pay. In fact, the businesses themselves are magnets for lots of folks who want to make a lot of money and who know how to sell, even if they know little about how to protect or grow their own or other people's money. Still, many will continue to consider themselves "experts." Yet many (but not all, of course) of those "experts" are just marketers. And that's why I want you to be especially careful about paying others to help you manage your money.

It is my opinion that, if you want to, and if you're willing to put in some time, study, and discipline, you too can learn enough about this stuff to do right by yourself and your hard-earned money.

And who knows? You might get really good at it. And like it, too.

THE MARKETING OF FUNDS

10

FUNNY, ISN'T IT, *how much supposedly "impartial" journalism turns on finding a* ***hook***—

something that will grab readers or viewers and rivet their attention.

On a slow news day, a little ice storm causing a few fender benders may be recast as:

The Storm of the Year!
Winter temperatures PLUNGING into the 20s!
We're there for you! Film at 11!

In the world of journalism, a rather vulgar maxim screams, "If it bleeds, it leads."

I'm not writing here, of course, about political spin

or press bias. I'm trying to help real people save, protect, and grow real money for their looming retirements. But really, I wish all personal financial journalists avoided sensationalism and took their responsibility to *help us understand* more seriously. You may not realize it, but some financial journalists are themselves learning on the job. Many others, however, should know better. So too, I wish the mutual fund people themselves—those people and their firms with whom we invest and who are supposed to help us save for our futures—treated us better than just . . . well, like fish to be reeled in.

You may not realize it, but the mutual fund business struggles with BIG-time conflicts of their own. On one hand, they want to make huge pots of money for themselves; yet on the other hand, they're supposed to help people invest intelligently. Whether you see the inherent conflict or not, believe me, it's not possible to do both well. One goal will inevitably suffer, and that one usually has to do with the investor. The mutual fund business is torn between providing fiduciary services to people hoping to steward their retirement funds AND also being successful marketing machines that gather assets and collect all the fees they can. Unfortunately, too many mutual funds side first with the profit-making side of their business, not the fiduciary side charged with helping you and me.

Does this really matter?

You betcha!

Let me give you an example of how much it matters, plucked fresh from what's going on in one mutual fund right now. This seemingly small example speaks loudly of the tension that exists between investors—who can get hurt, if they are not careful—and mutual fund managers looking after their own bank accounts. In this example, a famous mutual fund manager farmed out the management of one of his own funds to a less-famous, but very successful manager. The less-well-known manager, eager to make more money and gain more exposure for herself, took on the contract with the more famous boss. Time passed. The subcontractor did a great job. In fact, her performance proved stunning. By now, the successful manager was collecting a 4% load (remember, that's a sales charge) on any money coming into "his" fund (though managed by someone else)—plus, on top of that, collecting an additional 1.75% a year in management fees.

Before your eyes glaze over with those numbers, let me help you understand.

If we imagine a $10,000 investment made by you

into the celebrity manager's fund—managed by some-body else—before a dime of your money was invested, a 4% sales charge ($400 of your money) would have been lopped off, leaving $9,600 to be invested in the excellently performing fund. Then, every year you re-main invested, you would give up another $175 (plus or minus), depending on fund performance, to compen-sate the rich and famous manager who's actually paying a pittance to the subcontractor to manage your money.

By the way, you might want to recall what I said in chapter 4 about what the Vanguard Group charges for their investment work: in total, about $1.80 per year per $1,000, or $18.00 per year per $10,000 on a similar investment. Compare that charge with the $575 ($400 + $175) per $10,000 the big shot charges in year one, or even with the $175 he charges every year thereafter.

We all tend to acquaint paying more with getting a better product. High prices often signal better quality. Maybe that's true for shovels or necklaces, but it's not true with mutual funds. In fact, high-priced mutual funds are very often associated with poorer perform-ance, because the fund's results have to overcome a higher hurdle imposed by the higher fees.

I don't know what you'll choose, but I know where I'll invest my money.

Come on! Taking $400 in the first year and $175 each year after is, I think, a form of highway robbery tucked away in a mutual fund. But hey, it's entirely legal. Because the fees were fully disclosed in the prospectus—that legal document that tries to explain the goals and the inner workings of a mutual fund— even if investors did not understand what they were reading, or take the time to read it in the first place. Besides, no one held a gun to their heads to make them invest their money.

Most people just don't know about this kind of stuff. They don't understand, and sometimes they don't even seem to care. They don't do the necessary reading or comparison shopping in choosing their investments that they might do in choosing their cell phone.

And, remember, given the conflicts under which mutual fund marketers work, they are not in business to help you sort out this kind of information. You have to know what to ask (which is, I hope, where this book comes in).

So here's my first point on the marketing of mutual funds. Mutual fund companies are in business to make money. Consequently, my second point is: they are not always in business to help you invest in the right stuff at the right price.

Too many times, in fact, mutual fund companies may recommend things to you that you should NOT be investing in as opposed to things that you should be considering. Much too often what drives the marketing of mutual funds is what's "hot" at the moment—that is, what has recently done well in the market place. If, say, technology stocks have been on a tear, then the fund company may well direct your attention to its technology fund's record. If it's investments in the Far East—or commodities—that have wowed the markets, then, when you open your quarterly statement, don't be surprised if a slip of paper falls out suggesting the Far East or commodities as places you might well want to put some money.

This self-serving process encourages many unsophisticated, individual investors to chase hot-performing mutual funds, which is, I assure you, a recipe for disaster. Visions of excess returns—like 25% a year—start dancing in people's heads. Moreover, unsophisticated investors often have little perspective or the personal discipline to hunker down with a prudent selection of funds that, over time, will return something like 8–10% per year, when right now the "hot" fund may be making 20% a month!

Pursuing "hot" funds is so dangerous that I'm going

to spend more time on this topic in the next chapter.

In the meantime, remember: mutual funds provide an array of good and not-so-good funds. Be careful if you read ads or listen in on discussions of what is doing especially well this season—or this year. The hot funds may well be funds that have, recently, done very well—so well, in fact, that they are now due for a strong, negative correction. Use some judgment when it comes to investments. Or, if you have no judgment in fund selection, develop some. Quickly!

Once again: Wherever possible, invest in low-cost, no-load index funds as I recommended in chapter 4. These funds will not always—or even very often—lead the performance charts. But they should give you long-term success and fewer regrets, which is what saving for retirement is largely about.

In the investment world, as in life, if something sounds too good to be true, it most likely is.

CHASING PERFORMANCE

11

and Performance Monitors

ODD *though it may seem, chasing performance in a mutual fund is something you don't want to do.*

What I mean is, let go of the insane idea that whatever fund was "hot" last year will be hot again this year.

on't chase THAT fund or, if you're already in it, don't buy more of it.

Chasing performance fits squarely into the category of "a Big No-No."

"Hot" funds are so . . . well, last year. Yes, they did well in the past, especially the recent past. But then they become something like "crack" for many inexperienced investors—and even for some who are very experienced. These funds are hard to resist, given last year's performance, which puts them right up there at the very tippy-top of all 87 ba-zillion mutual funds you might invest in. But face it, you missed it. Too bad.

Now, let it go. Get on with life.

The best-performing funds during any prior period fill a teeny-tiny niche of the entire universe of mutual funds. As I am writing this, in the dismal investment climate of early 2008, last year's really hot performers were funds that invested in Russia, Latin America, precious metals, and in oil.

One fund, concentrated in Russia, was up 100% last year. Wow! Wouldn't it have been great to have had some of that in your retirement account? Absolutely! Often-times, however, when these hot funds began shooting out the lights, they were teenie-weenie funds with very few assets and very few shareholders. Then lightning struck! They got lucky, were in the right place at the right time, and the Niagara Falls of assets began flooding in. As more time passes, and as performance in their narrowly-focused area soars, the hot funds of the moment become investment vacuum cleaners, sucking in mega-bucks from people who want their own piece of the action.

But it's likely too late for you to jump in.

The fact is, "Johnny-come-lately" investors in hot funds often get their heads handed to them on a silver platter of reality. More often than not, last year's superfund becomes this year's recyclables left at the curb for pickup in the morning. Or, put another way, investors in the hot fund are likely to get hit by a financial 2x4 that pounds them upside the head with the fact that stocks rarely grow at the rate of 100% per year. And if they do, they don't do so for long. Yes, every year, a few do—but it's unlikely that any one will do so for more than a year!

Yet, just as a few people actually do win the lottery or have children who grow up to be rock stars, lots of people pursue the crazy fantasy that they, too, will hit the jackpot. "This year," they say, "with this fund, it will be different. I'm feeling lucky." And too many people keep plunking down their hard-earned retirement investment dollars into last year's hot funds.

Well, let them do it. But don't you do it.

Rarely, if ever, is the reason for last year's hot fund's performance the work of a guru with an unbelievable ability to see into the future and time things just right. Rather, the hot fund—and its manager—is the winner of an investing lottery.

In the investment world, never confuse luck with brains, even if some of us would rather be lucky than smart.

Stay instead with the widely-diversified mix of low-cost funds, mostly in stocks—US and non-US funds, some real estate funds, some very high-quality bond funds, and a tiny sliver of emerging markets stock funds. Everything else is dangerous—even if for a year or so it seems wildly attractive to inexperienced investors and becomes the darling of the financial press. Exceptionally good recent performance will keep luring people into dangerous funds they don't belong in.

So much for "hot" funds.

Then, too, there are mutual fund performance monitors out there, the most famous of which are firms like Morningstar and Lipper, who are supposed to follow mutual funds with an expertise that the rest of us can only dream about. Looking over their detailed tables and charts, categorizing winners and losers, we may begin to think, "If only I pay them their subscription fees, then I, too, will have the answers to the exam. I'll know what funds to invest in."

If only it were so simple!

But it's not, and never, ever will be. Both Morningstar and Lipper—and all their imitators—offer various amounts of good, sound investment advice, as well as helpful tools, to encourage us to make sensible choices. But unsophisticated investors expect too much of these services, seeing them as crystal balls. And for their part, the services themselves don't go far enough to discourage the craziness or the illusion that any of us —including them—can see into the future.

Technically, no honest fund monitor actually tells you that their system will pick next year's winners. But whether it's stars (which Morningstar uses) or rankings (which Lipper uses), fund monitors don't do enough to impress upon the unsophisticated investor the fact that *the stars and rankings are based entirely on past performance.* And past performance in the investment world, while important, does not often predict the future. In fact, if anything, exceptional recent performance may well be pointing to a correction coming up ahead.

People so much want to believe there is an "expert system" out there that, if only they pay the fee, will help them make foolproof choices in purchasing high-returning funds. No such system exists. But a well-diversified portfolio will give you about the best chance you can have of combining good returns with lower risks.

Whether it's a star system, a ranking, a proprietary timing formula, or a foolproof "numerical, evaluative, logarithmic adjustment paradigm"—they are all just guesses. Guesses most likely based on what funds have recently performed better than others. That's all they are. True, interviews with portfolio managers or analyses into the histories of decades ending with the digit "8" or ending in "0" may be fascinating. But so, too, are market performance correlations that link investment returns to women's skirt lengths or winners of the Super Bowl. All neat things to know and talk about around the water cooler. But, please, don't invest your money based on such things, no matter who's telling you about their "foolproof" system "that will get you into next year's hot fund 80% of the time." (The "foolproof" system will be fully divulged, by the way, only after you have paid the full subscription price of the newsletter.)

I question the value of all these "systems"!

You don't need them. And what's more, they aren't very helpful.

Neither you, they, nor I know what the future holds for our health, our lives, or our kids—let alone less important stuff like our investment portfolios.

So, again, I want to drive home to you this indisputable fact: holding anything other than a low-cost, well-diversified, equity-oriented mutual fund portfolio is . . . well, simply risking tomorrow's money on yesterday's information.

ANYBODY

12

for Some Free Money?

SURPRISINGLY, *there are lots of people who don't join their employer's payroll deduction retirement savings plans, be that plan a 401(k) or a 403(b).*

Studies show that the nonparticipation rate runs between 25 and 33% of all employees.

That's a lot of people who are passing up a really good thing.

Those not taking part do so, I guess, in order to "save" money for today and have more take-home pay. But almost always this is a big mistake. Such people may wind up not saving *any* money for retirement, which can make later life especially inconvenient. Such folks also don't seem to understand that they are, in many cases, passing up "free money" their employers are handing out to any and all who participate in their company's retirement savings plan.

There's no other way to say this: You simply *must* take part in your company's plan—and most especially if your employer is giving away money.

Here are a few very important things to understand about your company's retirement savings plan.

First, be sure you know the difference between a *pension plan* and a *profit-sharing plan*. A pension plan, which is also called a "defined-benefit" plan, tells you how much money per month you are going to get in retirement. In other words, the benefit is defined. If your company has a pension plan, then your employer (who's called the "sponsor") assumes the risks of coming up with the dough needed to take care of all the employees covered by their pension plan. Little wonder that in a globally-competitive business world, few American companies offer pension plans anymore. (One study, for instance, shows that pension and health benefits for retirees alone at General Motors now adds as much as $2,500 to the price of every vehicle GM makes.) And of the companies that still offer pension plans, many of them are terminating them.

On the other hand, profit-sharing plans (such as the 401(k) and the 403(b)) don't guarantee any level of retirement benefits. All they guarantee is that your employer will, if your employer earns a profit this year, make a contribution to your retirement account based on your pay. In other words, in the profit-sharing plan, it is the contribution—not the benefit—that is defined. (Please note, if your employer had no profits, then your employer doesn't have to make a contribution to the employees' defined-contribution plans.)

No doubt about it, defined-benefit plans are like animals on the endangered species list. Boy, oh boy, don't many of us wish that these things were still the rage. But they're not, though conscientious business executives are now offering us defined-contribution plans instead.

But as I say, these plans do not define the benefits we will get in retirement, a fact and a reality that troubles—even frightens—some. So much so, in fact, that some employees don't bother to join their workplace retirement programs, as if that might help provide better for later life. Yet defined-contribution programs are, for the most part, all we've got now in the workplace. But with some skill (and, hopefully, no perilously long-term downturns in the economy), an employee saving for retirement over many years might well do a whole lot better in a defined-contribution plan than he or she ever would have in a defined-benefit plan.

Which leads me back to the free money.

Years ago, when American companies supported pension plans, employees didn't have to learn how to manage their retirement savings or even think about making contributions to their retirement accounts. They *could* contribute if they wanted to, but whatever they contributed would merely supplement what was already coming their way by virtue of their employer's pension plan and Social Security benefits.

Today, however, working people *must* save for their own retirement years. And most for-profit, as well as many not-for-profit, enterprises will help their employees save some money for the future. In fact, many employers offer a "match" to your own contributions to help make your contributions grow faster. Some employers give dollar-for-dollar-matches. Some give a lump sum. Some give a lot if you first contribute a little— say, an employer might kick in 10% of your pay, if you first contribute 2%.

Whatever the level of the employer's match, it blows my mind that EVERYONE eligible doesn't take advantage of this free money. After all, it's yours for the taking. Even if you leave that company, you get to keep the money.

But if you do leave and take your retirement savings with you, please, oh *please*! don't spend it. Don't look at that money you've accumulated, maybe over years, in your 401(k) or 403(b) as some kind of piggy bank to buy a new Harley or new bedroom furniture or as a windfall to be blown in celebrating the fact that you no longer work for your tyrannical old employer.

That money is definitely not meant to be spent, played with, or wasted. You may have spent years building up what you now have. And if you continue to invest it and add to it through your next employer's retirement plan, you'll be that much closer to your retirement goal. Why blow it and have to start all over again? You'll set yourself back badly—and maybe have to pay additional taxes on it, too—if you spend what you've already accumulated for a cruise or a new car.

Instead, for the sake of your own future, take the money you get from your former employer's plan and roll it all over into your new employer's plan. Or, perhaps just as good, roll it over into an IRA, which I'll explain in chapter 13.

Happy saving!

YOU REALLY NEED AN IRA

13

An IRA, which stands for Individual Retirement Account, is a really neat thing.

I n 2008, IRAs let you save up to $5,000 a year—$6,000 if you're over 50. All money contributed to an IRA, along with whatever your IRA may earn, remains untaxed as long as the money remains in the IRA. In fact, you might never have to pay tax on your IRA once the money is in.

IRAs are not, however, things you can always set up at work. But that's not a problem. If you're unable to set up your IRA at work, you might consider going to a low-cost fund group like Vanguard (www.vanguard.com) or TIAA-CREF (www.tiaa-cref.org) to open your IRA. I mention those two firms only because they have a nice selection of funds with decent returns, while being trustworthy and inexpensive.

But really, you need an IRA. In fact, unless you are independently wealthy, you should have both an IRA and a 401(k) (or 403(b)).

So open up an IRA and fund it! Now!

Preferably with a good, low-cost, no-load (meaning no sales charge) mutual fund company. To make sure you get the right mix of assets, check back to chapter 7 for the kinds of funds you should have—US stock, US Treasury bonds, international stock, and so forth—and what percentage of each you should invest in. Keep in mind the overall percentages of assets you have in each of the asset classes I've recommended, and balance these percentages among all of your various investments. Your IRA might be a good place to put some US Treasury bonds or real estate money, rather than your stock funds, because both bonds and real estate tend to produce income that would be taxable outside of the protective environment of a tax-deferred IRA.

And why should you open an IRA?

Every year, the folks at the Social Security Administration put out estimates of where the "average" retiree is getting his or her money from. Recent figures tell us that about 39% of the average retiree's income is coming from Social Security payments; a whopping 24% is coming, post-retirement, from some kind of job; 16% is coming from the retiree's own outside investments; and about 9% is coming from pension plans. (Yup! Some people are still drawing money from those neat old things.) These figures don't total 100%, but they cover most of the average retiree's income—at least in the eyes of the Social Security Administration.

Do you follow what this means?

Today, the bulk of retirees' income comes from four sources.

Do you have four sources of income for YOUR retirement?

Three?

How about two?

This is where an IRA comes into the picture to supplement your retirement income.

So, please, for your sake—and the sakes of your spouse and your other loved ones—don't ignore an IRA. It can really help, especially if you begin one when you're young. For example, a single $5,000 contribution to your equity-oriented IRA made 35 years before you retire could reasonably grow to $53,000 without any further contributions.

Importantly, there are two different kinds of IRAs. One kind, the "traditional IRA," offers you a tax deduction <u>before</u> your money goes in. Your money then grows until retirement without being taxed. Once you're in retirement, as you withdraw your money, only then do you pay taxes on everything that comes out—that is, both your contributions and whatever they earned over the years they were invested.

A traditional IRA is a good way to save for retirement. And, as an extra bonus, for contributing to a traditional IRA (if your income isn't too big) you also get a current year's tax deduction on your contribution.

But wait! There may be an even better IRA for you —the Roth IRA. Like the traditional IRA, money put in a Roth grows without being taxed. But, unlike a traditional IRA, a Roth IRA doesn't give you a current-year's tax deduction when your money goes in. Instead—and maybe lots better—the Roth IRA lets you take your money out, in retirement, tax-free. Whoo-hoo!

Imagine that! No taxes later on! Wow! What a great idea! And it's all yours for the taking.

Roth IRAs are not available, under current rules, to people who make more than about $150,000 a year. But that leaves lots and lots of us to qualify for its generous, tax-free benefits. If you work, and you make money doing so, you (or your spouse) qualify for one of these two types of IRAs—maybe both. So open one. You need to.

Both of these IRAs have various income, withdrawal, and age limitations that you should understand before you invest. But don't miss the great opportunity you have to enhance your own future retirement because, today, you're going out to dinner too often. Or buying a new car. Or putting in a kitchen that will cause others to drool. None of that will have been worth it if you're down to your last nickel at age 85, waiting for the soup kitchen to open.

Also—and listen up now!—there is something else out there, still quite new, to help you save even more for your future. And it's more powerful than either of the IRAs I've just mentioned.

I'm talking about Roth 401(k) plans. Or, if you work for a not-for-profit, they're called Roth 403(b) plans. Both of these programs require enrollment through your workplace. So ask your employer if you have one, and don't ignore yours if you do. On the other hand, if your employer doesn't yet have one, ask when it's coming.

Here's how they work.

If you've read this far, you'll probably remember that I wrote about 401(k) and 403(b) plans back in chapter 11, "Anybody for Some Free Money?" There, I pleaded with you NOT to pass up your employer's generous offer to pay you to join the company's retirement plan. No kidding, free money really is being given away. But it's usually given away only if you first put some of your own money into the plan.

Well, ordinary 401(k) and 403(b) plans operate much like traditional IRAs but with considerably higher contributions permitted. Your money goes in untaxed, grows tax-deferred, then comes out—ideally, only when you retire. And, as the money comes out, only then is it taxed. Lots of people think that in retirement they will be in a lower tax bracket. But who knows? Just remember, your 401(k) or 403(b) will be taxed only as you withdraw from it in your retirement years. But taxes then could be higher than today.

Now consider the new Roth 401(k) or the Roth 403(b). Like the regular Roth IRA, your money goes in on an after-tax basis and comes out, hopefully years later and much larger, tax free. But while a regular Roth IRA currently has a $5,000 ($6,000 if 50 or over) maximum contribution limitation per year, the Roth 401(k) and 403(b) have $15,500 ($20,500 if 50 or over) limitations per year, NOT including money your employer may also throw in as a match. The new Roths are outstandingly good retirement savings vehicles for employees at least 10 years from retirement, and the younger you are, the more meaningful they could be to your retirement.

Come on now, if your workplace has a Roth 401(k)—or a Roth 403(b)—and you're <u>not</u> yet 55, why aren't you contributing to it?

And if your workplace doesn't yet have one, ask your employer to look into setting one up.

The new Roths are just too good to pass up.

MEN AND WOMEN AND INVESTING

14

MANY *of us may remember, way back when we were kids,*

taking long drives in the summer on family vacations.

oy, oh boy, I can remember being in the back of the car in the days before air conditioning —let alone in-car DVD players—and wondering out loud, "When will we EVER get there?" Mom or Dad, taking pity on us little people, might see a billboard along the way and point out the "Mystery Spot" or "The Ripley's Believe It or Not Museum" up the road, just another hundred miles. And to break up the monotony—or maybe to keep themselves from being driven crazy— Mom and Dad would mercifully get off the highway and give us a break from the seemingly endless trip.

In my growing up, I remember a Tepee Motel in Winslow, Arizona; a cast-concrete, walk-in alligator in central Florida; the splendid excesses of "South of the Border" in South Carolina; and yes, that Mystery Spot in upstate New York that, once visited, I was sworn not to tell anyone about.

Well, look at this chapter as a little break from the monotony of the retirement investment interstate. The Mystery Spot didn't wind everyone's watch, of course, but for some, strangely, it became the highpoint of their whole vacation.

So let's pull off the highway, turn down a side road, and have a little discussion about men, women, and investment.

Is there any research on this subject?

You'd better believe it. And two points stand out.

Research tells us that, in general, men and women invest differently, and show different tolerances for risk taking. First, women tend, generally, to be less charmed by risk-taking, and, second, they tend to rely more on the advice of people they feel know more about investing than they do.

This doesn't mean that ALL women fear taking risk, nor that all men jump at the chance to take more risks. But the research conclusions tend in that direction.

Why? Perhaps we'll save that discussion for a book I will never write, something like *The Shortest Guide Ever to Differences Between the Sexes* . . . but let me offer some thoughts about this Mystery Spot.

While these research findings about the investment tendencies of men and women can easily be overstated, my own experience working with wealthy clients reminds me again and again that men tend to be more comfortable taking risks. (And investing is, after all, a lot about learning how to take some intelligent risks.)

Women, for many reasons, may tend to be the more conservative sex. That doesn't make them "bad" investors. In fact, successful investing means more than just learning to take risks. It also requires learning that, sometimes, "not losing is winning," which women seem to understand more intuitively than men. Still, there are two aspects of risk taking and sex that are very important to explore.

First, let's consider the implications for long-term investing if women actually are more conservative investors.

As I've said, in my money management work with clients over many years, I certainly found my female clients to be more conservative investors. But remember, if we are investing for the short term, a conservative orientation is absolutely the right route to take. If money is needed for next month or even next year, DON'T take risks at all. In fact, use a savings account, a money market account, or maybe a one-year CD.

But . . . retirement investing is NOT about saving for next year. It's about saving for the long term—indeed, the VERY long term. In some cases that's 20, 30, or even 50 years out. Here, an investor's discomfort with taking intelligent risk can be a major liability, whether we're talking about males or females.

However, since the right thing to do for the short term is not the right investment for the long term, women who hate to take risks put themselves at a considerable disadvantage for their long-term retirement. The more conservative a woman is, the harder it will be for her to capture the bulk of investment returns only equity-oriented investments can offer.

As mentioned in earlier chapters, stocks historically return about 10% per year over the long term. (Note that I say "the long term." That means 10 to 30 years or more.) Don't count on a largely equity-oriented portfolio returning 10% in any one year among, say, the 40 years that comprise the investment horizon for a typical retirement investor. The compound average return (which means the additional interest or dividends or growth earned on your original investments), may well turn out to be 10%, but the individual yearly returns, over a 40-year span, may run anywhere from negative 20% to plus 50% in any given year. To get the average of 10% per year over the long term, the retirement investor has to be able to stomach the sometimes gut-wrenching roller coaster of ups and downs that will likely, in time, average out at about 10% per year.

Follow what I'm saying?

The retirement investor who isn't comfortable enough taking investment risks—who can't stand the inevitable volatility involved in investing—needs to learn how to take some appropriate risks over a few decades of investing, if she (or he) has any hope of getting reasonable returns from their investments. For, make no mistake about it, an investor can't, and won't, get 10% per year by buying CDs or investing in a money market fund (unless future inflation eats us all alive). True, with those kinds of low-risk investments, very conservative people may sleep better while they're saving for retirement. But once in retirement, those same souls—whether they are men or women—may be up many a night tossing and turning from fear of running out of money.

So, my dear conservative ladies (and, yes, overly

conservative gentlemen too), please: if you're very, very risk averse, try to learn how to take some intelligent risks with your retirement investments. As a start, read over the principles I have laid out in this book and put most of the money you are saving for retirement into an equity-oriented portfolio.

OK?

Now we're almost done with our short excursion off the beaten path. Just one more point before we get back in the car to finish up our journey. And that point has to do with advisors and conservative investors.

Conservative retirement investors may well, as I've already said, turn to others to help them manage their retirement money. And if they do so, they must be very careful about the advisors they pick.

Most advisors working with women, for instance, know that women are less enamored with risk taking, so their advisors may avoid suggesting the very assets female clients need in their retirement investment port-folios. Instead, to keep a client from feeling uncom-fortable, which could threaten a profitable business relationship, the advisor may recommend very conser-vative retirement investments. Yet, by doing so, fearful investors' biases are reinforced rather than gently challenged. With the difficult education avoided, the overly conservative investor does not learn how to invest for the long term (meaning, how to create a largely equity-oriented portfolio).

Of course, not all advisors with very conservative clients will duck the challenges of trying to get them to learn how to take some risks. But some *will* duck the challenge in order to keep their clients happy today. After all, advisors are in business to collect fees, not to push clients in directions they don't want to go, however helpful or sensible that new direction could be.

Now, enough of the Mystery Spot. Everybody back in the car. We've still got some miles to go before we get to Grandma's.

TO ANNUITIZE OR NOT?
That Is the Question

COME *retirement, you'll have to make a very big decision.*

Do I, or don't I, turn my retirement savings plan into an annuity?

An annuity is an amount of money that is paid to you on a regular basis. Pension plans of days gone by are great examples of annuities. Once an employee retired, his or her old employer cut a check for them every month—for life!

Social Security is another example of an annuity. Month after month, as long as a retiree and his or her spouse shall live, there's a check in the mailbox (or at the bank, if the recipient uses direct deposit, which, by the way, I HIGHLY recommend).

Just about everybody's workplace retirement savings

plan offers an annuity option into which you can save and from which you can withdraw your money once you retire.

I get asked a lot, "Should I annuitize my retirement savings?"

Well, like many other answers to hard questions in life . . . it depends.

First, let's make sure we understand what is involved if you do choose to annuitize your retirement savings. Annuitizing will occur ONLY at that moment when you enter retirement and you start getting those monthly checks. It does not occur at any other time, say, when you're still working and accumulating money into your retirement plan. That long period of time—when you're saving up—is called the "accumulation" period. That's the time when you're still working and your money is being saved—or accumulated—for later, possible, annuitization.

To turn your accumulated retirement savings plan into an annuity and thereby start getting a series of life-long checks, you will have to make an irreversible decision. If you annuitize, you contract with an insurance company to give you lifetime income every month—or, if you choose, every quarter or year. By so doing, you give up your right to whatever might be left over when (not if) you die. Be certain you understand this: Whatever is left over in your retirement savings account once it has been annuitized belongs, not to your kids, your favorite charity, your volunteer fire department, or possibly even your spouse. It belongs to the insurance company with whom you contracted to receive your lifetime annuity.

Whether you realize it or not, an annuity is a kind of bet you make with an insurance company. You bet you're going to live a long time, and the insurance company bets you won't. You transfer the risk of living a long time to the insurance company, and they accept that risk largely for the chance to take over what's left in your retirement savings plan after you die. You live a long time, you win, because the insurance company is obligated to make payments to you as long as you live—even if those payments exceed the amount of money you initially annuitized. You die early, they win, because they keep whatever remains of your savings account.

Companies that write annuity contracts know that such bets would be stupid if made with just a few people. But when these bets are made by insurers with tens of thousands of annuity holders, the large numbers create a surprising amount of certainty for the insurance company. They don't know who will die early and who late, but they can price their benefits based on the overall population that buys their annuities.

Rest assured, however, there are some specific ways —at a cost—under most annuity contracts to ensure that your spouse gets annuity payments for the rest of his or her life. Alternatively, at a different cost, you may provide up to, for example, 10 years of payments after your death to your spouse or to someone else. In other words, in the latter case, if you should die four years into retirement, and you had chosen to annuitize your retirement savings account—and you checked the right box on the contract—your spouse would receive another six years of annuity payments. (That is, four years of payments, while you were alive, *plus* six more years of payments after your death, equal 10 years of total annuity payments.)

But after that, it's Good-bye, money.

If an annuity option exists within your workplace retirement plan, you can invest directly in it and receive interest on your investments during your working years, sort of like a CD at a bank. Then, at retirement, you can choose to annuitize (or not annuitize) whatever you have accumulated. On the other hand, you or other employees may have been putting money away in, say, equity-oriented mutual funds in your workplace retirement

111

plan. At retirement, you and the others, just like those who had all along been saving their money in the plan's annuity option, will be able to convert their accumulated savings into an annuity, should they wish to.

In many cases the savings an employee accumulates under an annuity (especially a "fixed" annuity, which is what most annuity purchasers buy) will often give the employee a lower long-term rate of return on their accumulated savings than if the employee's money had been invested in an equity-oriented mutual fund portfolio.

Annuities also tend to be very expensive savings vehicles because they carry investment, sales, administrative, and insurance expenses. So, at retirement, you might not have as much money as you might have had if you had used no-load mutual funds as your savings vehicles. Moreover, with a fixed annuity, your monthly payments in retirement will be based on what your account balance was at the time you retired, not later on, even though your money continues to earn more for the insurance company.

It's quite possible, in other words, that you might well have done better without the annuity. BUT you would have had to live with the uncertainty of not knowing how much your retirement savings would give you on a regular basis for the rest of your life.

On the other hand—let me be very frank—if you are a timid soul, you might *not* have done better on your own, since to do better you'd have to invest on your own without an annuity contract (guaranteeing a monthly check). And you might have invested too conservatively.

Even with all their drawbacks—at least, in my opinion —some people still find annuities very comforting, offering them peace of mind in the knowledge that they will have a guaranteed, predictable amount of monthly income. For life!

And please understand: Anyone who tells you that investing is only about producing the highest return on your money is simply ignorant of the facts. Good investment is about achieving the highest rate of return consistent with the goals and risk-tolerance the investor has. If all this investment stuff causes you to lose sleep —like the kid in high school who freaks out over his math problems—an annuity ain't half bad.

Still, to me, they cost too much and, if you die early, often take too much from your family. But that's me, not you. You're the one who will need to sleep at night with the choice you make. And if you will sleep better with an annuity, regardless of the cost, then by all means, get an annuity.

However, for those of us who want to create on our

own something in retirement very similar to an annuity, even if it's not "guaranteed" by an insurance company, there are ways to do that.

"Like how?" you may wonder.

Like, first, by arriving at retirement with a healthy amount of money, saved and grown from a well-diversified portfolio of investments (there's that equity-oriented portfolio again that I keep recommending) or from a lifecycle fund. Upon your retirement, you can tell the mutual fund company managing your retirement fund—let's call it Fidelity, Vanguard, or TIAA-CREF—not to annuitize your accumulation. Just let it continue to be invested as it is, and that you now want to begin to withdraw from your portfolio under what's called a "systematic withdrawal plan," and NO MORE THAN 4% per year.

"And please send me a check, every month."

But no more than 4% per year, got it? (Promise me!)

"Why 4%?" Because many academic studies in finance involving simulation exercises tell us that at a withdrawal rate of 4% per year, a largely equity-based portfolio, returning about 8–10% per year over the long term, will have an 89% chance of not being depleted in 30 years—a reasonable amount of time, taking you out to 95 years of age (that is, if you retire at 65).

BUT! (Uh-oh! Hear the sirens? See the flashing red lights!?)

But, if you take out 5% a year, the likelihood of 30-year depletion significantly increases. In that case, the finance professors are only 63% sure that your portfolio will last 30 years. And above a withdrawal rate of 5%? Well, at that rate your portfolio might just as well be called a cookie jar on the kitchen counter being raided for lunch money.

For myself—and maybe you—I'm more confident that I can do a better job living off my own money in retirement and having money left over after my death to give to family and charity than I am in an annuity "guaranteed" by an insurance company. But please understand, we each have to think through the issue for ourselves.

Also, you may have noticed that I've used quotation marks around the word *guaranteed*. That was not an accident. I don't want to make light of the "guarantee" that an annuity company—that is, an insurance company—provides to an investor. Those guarantees are real, and, for the most part, they are very good. But remember that you may be receiving payments in retirement from that insurance company over a long, long time—maybe 30 or 40 years, I hope. Yet that guarantee extends to you only from the particular insurance company who has contracted to provide you with a lifetime, retirement annuity. Should they fail sometime in the future—say 26 years into your retirement—that could spell big trouble for you.

Such things can happen, even if they rarely do. Yet, in such cases, you may not get any more retirement income checks in your mailbox.

Again, such breakdowns are rare indeed. But they have happened. Back in the 1980s, for instance, a formerly-successful piano company, whose piano-making business was not as exciting as its owners had hoped, got itself into the financial services business, which at the time seemed a lot hotter and more profitable than making musical instruments. And, as luck would have it, this piano-turned-annuity company became one of America's hottest annuity sellers.

At least, for a while.

Indeed, Baldwin United was a big deal.

And then, all of a sudden, it was a big mess. In fact, it got itself—and its annuity holders—into really big trouble. So big that it could no longer pay the promised monthly benefits it had committed to pay to many, many people who had bought its annuities. Back then, some of us wondered, a bit uncharitably I suppose, if the annuity holders might be offered a piano instead.

I don't want to leave you with the thought that what happened to Baldwin United and to its annuity clients is a common outcome, because it certainly isn't. In fact, annuity companies—like insurance companies—are evaluated constantly by insurance raters, such as A. M. Best and Company. These raters assign letter grades, just like in school. And the best grade is—you guessed it—"A+."

If you go the annuity route, make sure you check the insurance company's rating. Get that rating in writing. Don't accept any company's salesperson telling you, "I'll check it out for you, but I think it's an 'A.'" Don't accept any company rated less than "A," even if they may offer you a little more money a month than you would get from an A-rated company. This is not an area where you—or someone advising you—will want to overreach, getting a few more bucks a month by taking on higher risks. That could be disastrous.

So to answer our original question about whether or not to annuitize . . . I guess you can, if you feel you need to and don't mind paying more for the privilege. But you may wish to explore all your other options first. And then, if you still want to annuitize, go ahead and do it. But be careful. Very careful.

INVESTING WITH A CONSCIENCE

HOW WE SPEND *and invest our money reveals a whole lot about who we are and what we hold dearest.*

Today, the investment world offers us lots of choices if we want to save money while supporting companies and causes we believe in.

The investment world now offers us dozens of "socially responsible" or "socially conscious" mutual funds. In fact, by some calculations, socially responsible investing is, right now, the fastest growing segment of money-under-investment management. The Social Investment Forum, an organization in Washington, D.C., that keeps track of these issues, says that, as of early 2007, more than $2.2 trillion—or about one in every $10 under management—was invested with an eye toward satisfying investors' consciences.

Clearly, today, environmental issues have become a central focus of socially conscious investors. But so, too, over the years, have issues such as peace and justice, munitions production, sex and gender issues in the workplace, abortion and anti-abortion, and many others aroused the souls of people who invest. It's fair to say, I think, that there is no shortage of issues that move the consciences of those willing to put their money where their beliefs are.

And that is, at least in my view, a big part of the problem for socially responsible investing.

Today, there are over 100 funds available to investors interested in socially conscious causes. In addition to those I mentioned above, there are funds that focus on human and animal rights, nuclear power, gambling, community building, and shareholder activism. While many socially conscious mutual funds are run by smaller mutual fund companies, not likely available to you through a payroll-deduction, work-based retirement program, some larger fund groups also have a socially responsible fund offering. So, one way or another, if you really want to invest with your conscience, you'll be able to do that either inside or outside your employer's workplace retirement plan.

Still, I'm not convinced that these funds offer much to those who mean to do good.

Being the ornery sort of no-nonsense investor that I am, if you really want to go the socially responsible route, I wish you the very best. But I'm not putting in any of my money.

Why not?

Well, I have three reasons: costs, performance, and let me just call my third reason integrity.

First, costs. Socially responsible funds tend to charge higher fees than I'd like to see investors pay. Remember, as a sort of benchmark, that Vanguard's S&P 500 Index Fund charges about 0.18% per year, while— let me pick a larger, better known conscience fund—the Domini Social Equity Fund charges 1.19%. In fact, a 2003 study done at the University of Chicago, looking at more than 50 socially conscious funds, found these funds charged 0.2% more a year than non-conscience-based funds. Two-tenths of 1% may sound like chicken feed, but over time it's not. After all, 0.2% is more than the management fee of the Vanguard S&P 500 Index Fund for an entire year.

Performance, too, has not favored socially conscious funds. That same University of Chicago study I mentioned looked at 849 funds, of which 50 were socially conscious, and all of which had been open at least three years. Among those 50 socially responsible funds there were prohibitions against investing in a wide array of things, including businesses that deal in liquor, tobacco, gambling, nuclear power, the nation's defense, and in the case of religious funds, drug companies that make the abortion pill and abortion supplies. Please understand, not each fund had the same set of restrictions.

The University of Chicago study found a performance gap between the 50 socially responsible funds and the 799 other funds. Socially conscious funds, over the three years in question, underperformed their non-conscience-driven competitors by 0.3% per month, or about 4.3% per year, including compounding. Another study, this one by Morningstar Inc., the mutual fund monitoring organization, done even more recently, compared socially conscious US funds with the broader S&P 500. It found the socially conscious funds lagged in their returns 8.53% vs. 10.32%, per year, for the S&P 500, for the three years ending in 2006. And while the Morningstar study also looked out over the prior 10 years and found the performance gap narrowed a bit (to 7.21% per year vs. 7.93% for the S&P 500), results still, favored the non-conscience-driven funds.

A recent University of Pennsylvania study involving

a still longer time period came to a similar conclusion.

In fairness, however, to the many people who really want to invest with their consciences, there is some encouraging news. I've seen some other studies, similar to those I've mentioned, coming not from America but from Australia, Canada, Germany, Japan, and England, and each of these studies comes to somewhat different conclusions. These foreign studies conclude that socially conscious funds, for the most part—at least in their respective lands—neither outperformed nor underperformed their less-conscience-driven competition.

Third, as for "integrity," I'm concerned that, in the end, even beyond costs and performance, investors in socially conscious funds may not get what they're paying for. Let me explain.

One of the bedrock principles of prudent investing, and one which I've tried to drill deeply into the hearts and minds of my readers, is diversification. It's absolutely essential to good investment management. Diversification is a miracle invention that reduces an investor's risks without offsetting their performance significantly. Now, if I take that principle and apply it to socially conscious investing—and, just for argument's sake, let's say to environmentally-conscious investing—how does a conscience-driven fund avoid concentrating its assets in too narrow a group of environmental companies, many of which may also be very small and unable to accommodate large infusions of investor money?

For instance, how much money can environmentally conscious funds collectively put into, say, companies that engage in organic foods or solar power? Indeed, the companies doing those sorts of things are, themselves, quite small. And if my fund tries to get around this size problem by investing in larger companies—say, General Electric, which has a meaningful wind turbine business —then, whether I like it or not, I also pick up GE's jet engine business, which makes engines for commercial airliners.

But also for jet fighters.

And a socially conscious investor may not mind the engines made for airlines, yet abhor the engines manufactured for jet fighters, because of their harmful potential.

Another problem arises if the socially conscious fund grows. It will need to find more companies, and bigger companies, in which to invest, some of which might take the fund beyond its narrow area of social responsibility. Also, competitive pressures lead many socially conscious funds to buy into businesses that are, well, merely doing well. This can lead the socially responsible fund to look an awful lot like the S&P 500

123

Index, with some tweaking around the edges to give investors a little bit of socially conscious activities, such as an investment in solar power or microfinance loans.

Another problem can come up if you're trying to fit your own conscience into the conscience of a mutual fund. The two don't always mesh. For instance, an investor may seek a mutual fund that supports equality of the sexes in the workplace. However, such a fund may also support gay rights, which the same investor may or may not also wish to support.

You catch my drift? The world we live in is a very murky place. How can one make investment decisions where the choices are so muddled? Where the standards are so fuzzy?

Want more examples of unavoidable confusion? Take nuclear power, which is, for socially conscious funds, a definite no-no because of the waste materials produced. Yet nuclear power generates electricity without emitting any greenhouse gases, even if it produces nuclear waste. Or, for a moment, let's consider a different slant on socially conscious investing. How do the managers themselves choose to live their lives? And should that matter?

For instance, I'm thinking of a couple of investors who manage mutual funds that are not considered socially conscious, yet who themselves lead personal lives that might well appeal to socially oriented investors. John Montgomery, for example, runs the small Bridgeway family of mutual funds, very likely too small to be among your choices for your payroll deduction retirement plan. But get this: Montgomery himself voluntarily limits his salary to a fraction of the investment industry average and gives half of his profits away to charity.

Or take the case of Don Yacktman, who runs some bigger funds—though still less likely to be available at your workplace. Don is a person of faith who doesn't smoke, swear, or drink anything stiffer than lemonade. His investment performance has put some of his funds at the top of their categories. Yet all the while, in pursuit of getting good investment results for his funds, Yacktman has unapologetically maintained huge investments in Altria Group, the parent of Philip Morris, the cigarette maker—another definite no-no to many socially conscious investors.

Neither Montgomery nor Yacktman run socially conscious funds, though their lives radiate, like heat from a stove, deep commitments to social and religious values. They simply believe that their investors, like themselves, will do best if they make as much money as they can and then, from their gains, write bigger checks to whatever charities they wish to favor.

I don't mean to say, or even suggest, that socially conscious investors are not seeking to do good. They are. I know that. But, personally, I prefer the paths Montgomery and Yacktman take in trying to help their investors help the world.

For those who might like to look at the large array of socially conscious investment options that are currently out there (spanning the political, social, and religious spectrum from liberal to conservative), you might want to check out the Web site of the Sensible Investor: http://www.sensibleinvestor.com/soconiment.html.

THE
GOOD NEWS
(and the Bad News)

THERE'S *good news and bad news about retirement.*

**The good news is that you're going to retire.
The bad news is that you're going to retire.**

The good news is that a time is coming when, after years of rushing and bustling, saving and scrimping, practicing discipline, and maybe praying it will arrive, you will finally get that great gift so few enjoy during their working years—the gift of time.

And it's humbling, I think, to realize that not many people in this world ever get that gift of time. But quite a few in our part of the world do. Even a lot of us who don't know what to do with it.

Ah! the gift of time!

Time during which you can do almost anything you

wish. Time to do things you've always wanted to do. Time to play golf or bridge, read, walk, sleep in, take trips, visit the kids or grandkids. Maybe time to work on projects you've dreamed about doing for years but never had time for.

I hope very much that when your retirement comes, you will have health and time to do everything you ever wanted to do. And I also hope you will have enough money to do those things.

My little book has focused on but one important part of the retirement puzzle: That part that deals with accumulating enough money to be able to retire without the proverbial wolf constantly scratching at your door.

But you know what? There's so much more to retirement than merely having enough money to retire. As someone who worked for years to help rich people grow and manage their money, I realize that many people want to make money to buy better cars or bigger houses or take fancier trips, as if these things will, finally, bring them life's joys. Lots of people make money and just spend it, giving little thought to anything beyond their own desires or fantasies.

But, frankly, I'm not at all sure that lots of stuff that we pursue will ever give us—or those we love—the deep down sense of contentment that we're all looking for. My experience tells me that too many people focus far too much of the best energies of their lives on money issues, because they see those things as most important. Most people in our culture believe that the more money they have, the happier they will be, and so devote most of their lives to accumulating as much as possible.

Once upon a time I was someone who lived a sort of "high life," and helped many others live theirs. In my old life, I was not infrequently invited into the confidences of many a client who, with millions under management, confided to me that they worried about not "having enough." My work was, after all, a lot about helping people achieve their dreams. But not a few of my clients worried about the state of their dreams. Yet I also worked, in a few cases, with people with much less money but who still found freedom and contentment in what they had.

I can tell you from personal experience that it wasn't wealth or possessions that ever gave me, or those I worked for, "lasting happiness"—or something like it. In many cases, I think they may have gotten in the way or blinded their possessors to other, more important, things.

I agree, yes, it is hard to live contentedly without a certain amount. But after some reasonable amount of money has been accumulated, getting more and more doesn't seem to add much to our happiness. And sometimes can even add to our anxiety, self-absorption, and discontent.

Saving enough money for retirement matters, but it isn't—I hope for you—what life or retirement is really all about. The bigger issue I hope that you will find time to address is, "What kind of person am I tending to become?"

Yes, even in retirement.

Ready or not, retirement is coming. <u>YOUR</u> retirement, too! And when it does it will wind up enveloping your whole life like a princely robe.

Or a wet blanket.

It can give you a new perspective on life and bring fresh insights into love, work, and investing in the lives of others. Or, if you're not ready, or careful, it could set you up for depression, shock, and disappointment.

Retirement will be for you, I hope, a doorway into a rich, new chapter of your life that will make everything that came before just necessary preparation. But the difference between retirement becoming the greatest time of your life rather than a bad dream will be due to more than luck or good health—or even money. It will also come from how you choose to <u>invest</u> the rest of your life.

Often it begins with our hobbies or involvements with others outside or inside our work life. But during our work lives, we may not have had the time or the means to get involved enough in these outside interests. Then suddenly, in retirement, the time is there. And maybe, if we're prudent (and blessed), we'll then have the time and some money to get involved in a whole new line of work, where making money or rising to the top is no longer as important, say, as helping kids read, getting heat for poor people's homes, or maybe using your skills and abilities to bless those in less developed countries.

If I may, let me tell you a little about my own life. I don't see myself as a great example in any way, but just someone who is trying to learn, grow, and develop in all that I might become. What I'm about to tell you is my story, of course, not yours. I'm not trying to fit your life into mine or suggest that you make the same choices I did. I never thought that I would become a college professor. But at age 46, I had a chance to take an 80% pay cut (who could pass that up?) and move from cosmopolitan Boston to small town Indiana (who could pass that up either?).

Why in the world would I have done something so crazy? And crazy is what some friends of mine back in

Boston thought it was. Well, for me, the reason arose about nine years earlier, with a very unexpected mid-30s change in my spiritual life. Simply put, I discovered I had one. In that discovery, I began to believe in God, and to take God seriously: in other words, as something (or someone) more than a curse word. And I began to see that whatever I had accomplished so far in life was not just because of me and for me. No, now I began to see so much of what I had been given as gifts from God. And in realization and out of gratitude, I wanted to return, if I could, to this world and to my God more than just the space I was taking up.

Almost immediately, I also began to say a certain prayer. It went something like, "Lord, please help me to use my gifts and talents to their highest and best use." I'm not sure, as a brand-spanking new believer in Jesus, that I actually thought my prayer would be heard. And if it were heard, I wasn't sure I'd know how to respond to what might come next. But in time, after having written and spoken a bit about the convergence of faith in my life and work, I was invited to speak at a little college in Indiana. You know, I was just supposed to come tell the students about what I did for a living and how Jesus had changed my life, even if not my job. So I went out there and did that. And then I went home to Boston.

But the president of that college in Indiana called me up a few months later and wondered if I might want to come teach business and economics. *Can't say that I do*, I thought. But then I remembered that prayer I'd been muttering over and over again, the one about wanting my "gifts and talents" used to their highest and best. And not long after that, I felt a kind of divine tug, if you know what I mean, to come and see. See if this was right for me, if this was a way I might use my gifts and talents, given to me by God, in a higher and better way.

It was my time to think about doing something else. I wasn't thinking at all about retirement. I didn't sense I *had* to make this move, either. No, not at all. It was just something offered to me to try, to do my best. But I sensed I had been given the gifts and experience that, with God's grace, might make it work.

That was fifteen years ago. Since then my new life has been filled with many challenges and adjustments, joys and disappointments. I was terrified we'd run out of money. But that just never materialized. Yet just months after arriving in Indiana, my wife was diagnosed with terminal cancer. It was a great blow, but thankfully she's still alive today. Then she needed a heart transplant. Mercifully, she got that too, and continues to do pretty well, giving a lot of her time to hospice work.

Life is not easy. Whether you live in a big city or a small town, great challenges will threaten you. Count on it.

But the choice we made to come to Indiana, take a large pay cut, and teach have been, I think, worthy of the time and life God has given me. My family feels so, too. Now, as I approach 60, I'm not all that far from retirement myself. I'll probably keep teaching as long as I have the strength and health, because I think I feel God's pleasure in teaching the next generation. I may have to cut back, but I don't need to know that just yet. For now, I'm just grateful to have the time and skills to do what I think is important and helpful in this very broken world.

Soon—or maybe even now—it will be YOUR time to choose, to choose what you will do next. Maybe your choices will be more limited than mine; for sure, you will have different ones set before you. However, one thing is for sure: you won't get your time back; you won't get to live it twice. And as you enter into or are now living through your retirement, you're also becoming something else, either something good or something less than what you might have hoped.

What are you tending to become? What is it that you want these summary years of your life to stand for and to say to those who will live on after you?

Funny, isn't it? In life or in retirement, oftentimes the more we focus on ourselves, the more we find we're bored or we're missing something or we've got aches and pains. On the other hand, the more we choose to focus on others and try to help them with their needs—be they grandchildren or a neighbor or needy people overseas— the more we tend to find, surprisingly enough, our own needs met.

And in the process, we become more generous, gracious, and fulfilled people.

THE END
(as Well as the Beginning)

18

IF YOU'VE GOTTEN *this far reading my little book, trying to educate yourself on how to manage a successful retirement savings plan, good for you.*

Congratulations!
But now it's time to go and do.

Reading won't matter if you don't take the steps I've outlined and summon the courage and discipline to follow through.

To help you remember what's important, keep these key points in mind:

▶ Remember, start early and keep saving. Save a lot. Persist. Save aggressively but invest prudently. Through thick and thin, keep investing. Keep it

up. No matter what. Don't expect it to be easy.
Spend less on lifestyle and foolishness.

Remember, the kind of investing that is right for a
savings goal one year away is NOT the right one if
you're investing for 30 years away—or even 10
years away.

Remember, in saving for retirement, develop an equity-oriented portfolio composed of a well-diversified mix of low-cost, no-load (that's no sales
charge), index funds, covering, if possible, US
stocks, foreign developed-market stocks, emerging
market stocks, real estate, and US Treasury issues.
Don't fret when your allocation to one of your
asset classes, say US stocks, isn't doing well. For it
will be very rare indeed that all your investments
will do well at the same time (or, for that matter,
be doing terribly at the same time).

Remember, pay attention to your investment expenses. You can't control your returns, but you can
control the costs you pay in pursuit of those returns. And don't feel, except to rebalance, that
you always have to do something: don't move

137

money around for no good reason, even if performance in one of your asset classes cools off.

▶ Remember, your goal should <u>not</u> be to "beat the market." It should be to capture as much of the return offered by the market as you can prudently get, which means taking only sensible risks. Another goal should be not to lose significantly in any year. However, do not expect your portfolio to rise every year. Over time, and with discipline, patience, and regular rebalancing of your portfolio, you should earn about 8–10% per year. Don't expect the asset classes I've suggested to grow at 16% a year. They will—sometimes. But not often. And when they do grow at 16% for a year or for a few years, EXPECT them then to UNDERperform for a time. Remember that at 8–10% per year growth, money doubles about every 7 to 9 years.

▶ Remember, over the long term of your retirement investing, there will be times when nothing seems to work, when markets tank, when no matter what you do, something seems wrong. When those times come, HANG ON. Ride them out. Continue to invest. Keep your asset allocation. Keep rebalancing.

Remember that this, too, shall pass.

▶ Remember, I hope—oh, boy, do I hope—that in your retirement years you will have more to look forward to than, say, just watching television (which happens to be the number one activity of retirees today). Or than just another golf date each morning or lemonade on the veranda in the late afternoon. Above all else, however, as you save money for your retirement—and you simply must do that!—think, explore, plan, dream, and perhaps pray about things you've always wanted to do, as well as things that might leave this world just a little better off for your having passed through. In other words, try to make a difference.

And ask yourself from time to time, "What kind of person am I becoming?"

GLOSSARY OF TERMS

401(k)—For those who work in for-profit businesses, a salary reduction plan that allows employees to defer current pay in order to contribute untaxed dollars to a tax-deferred retirement fund. Also, many times, employers match some part or all of an employee's contributions to help the employee's plan grow.

403(b)—Same as 401(k), but for those who work for NOT-for-profit organizations.

Annuity—A form of contract sold by an insurance company that guarantees a fixed or variable payment, often for life.

Asset—Anything having a commercial or exchange value: for example, your car or your house, if you have either, as well as the investments in your retirement plan.

Asset Allocation—Typically, the percentage of your assets (stocks, bonds, real estate, etc.) invested in each asset type (or asset class). No one asset allocation is right for all people nor for any one person throughout his or her life. Asset allocation reflects an investor's tolerance for risk, desire for growth or income, as well as the investor's age. Generally, older investors cut back on equity-oriented assets and add bonds.

Bond—An "I.O.U." issued by any number of organizations, including, for example, a company, a government, or a college. Bonds do not indicate ownership in the issuing organization, just a claim on some periodically paid interest income and, generally, the return of the amount initially invested.

Broker—An "intermediary" between an investor and his or her investments. Also called "Registered Representatives," "Investment Advisors," and "Investment Consultants," among other things. Brokers may (or may not) help you choose investments well. They may (or may not) calm your nerves. But brokers will, one way or another, be compensated for their work on your behalf.

Correlation—In investment work, correlation refers to the tendency of one type of asset to move in the same direction, at the same time, as another. Prudent investors seek investments for their retirement portfolios that do NOT correlate well.

Costs—The costs of investing are many and often hidden. Mutual funds charge you to manage your money. They also will add on expenses for meetings, printing, mailings, accounting fees, and lots else. Brokers—if you use one—have another layer of fees added on, including "loads," or sales charges, to buy shares in a mutual fund. Loads help compensate the broker. Mind your costs. Keep them LOW.

Defined-benefit Plan—An old-fashioned workplace retirement plan that provides for the retired employee an employer-paid monthly benefit. In other words, the benefit that the retired employee receives is *defined*, not the contribution that the employer paid to provide that benefit. Defined benefit plans are, increasingly, an endangered species; fewer and fewer remain.

Defined-contribution Plan—What most of us today have to help us save for retirement. In defined-contribution plans, the employer's contribution to the employee's retirement plan is *defined*, but not the benefit that may grow from that contribution. The employer's contribution is usually based on an employee's pay or on the profits of the employing company. Both 401(k) and 403(b) plans are defined-contribution plans.

Diversification—A very good thing! Diversification is the mix of different kinds of investments or asset classes (for instance, stocks, bonds, cash, real estate) held in a portfolio. You've probably heard the old saying that "it's dangerous putting too many eggs in one basket." Diversification refines that old saw a bit to say, "It's dangerous putting too many eggs of *one kind* in a basket." Diversification helps dampen an investor's risk, even as it also lessens an investor's "upside" potential. Yet, the reduction in risk is usually more profitable than the decrease in upside potential.

ETF—A newer type of "electronically-traded" indexed mutual fund that may be available to investors in some workplace retirement plans. ETFs usually have lower fees than regular mutual funds and can be traded throughout the day—the latter being a benefit of very questionable value to most sane investors.

Emerging Markets Funds—Mutual funds that hold investments in foreign countries that are growing rapidly; hence, such investments likely have good, long-term prospects of success. Currently, the major "emerging market" countries are referred to as the "BRICs"—Brazil, Russia, India, and China.

Equity-based Fund—Any type of mutual fund in which the fund's assets are invested in things that give a claim to investors on part of a corporation's assets and earnings.

Fund—In this book, shorthand for "mutual fund." See Mutual Fund.

Fund Monitor—Organizations that track news or performance of mutual funds. Today, the most recognized fund monitors are Lipper and Morningstar. While providing helpful performance statistics and management perspectives on mutual funds, monitors focus almost exclusively on past performance, since the future cannot be known.

Index Funds—A type of mutual fund in which the portfolio tracks the holdings of an index, such as the S&P 500 or the Dow Jones Industrial Average. Index investing is often considered to be "passive investing" because an index fund does not ask its portfolio manager to make any investment selections not already in the underlying index. Significant research and history shows that index funds are less expensive for investors and provide better-than-average returns than "actively" managed funds, in which a portfolio manager chooses the securities that comprise a fund's portfolio.

Inflation—The tendency, deeply embedded in almost all economies, for prices to rise over time. In America, the Consumer and Producer Price Indices (the CPI and the PPI) track prices. Updates to both are released monthly.

Lifecycle (or target-dated) Funds—A new type of mutual fund meant to help people make "one-step" decisions in saving for their retirements. Lifecycle funds are especially recommended for those people who are afraid of investing or who don't like to make investment decisions on their own. These funds invest in multiple asset classes (stocks, bonds, and cash, for instance) for investors who plan to retire at about the same time in the future. Then, over a period of many years, the lifecycle fund will automatically invest more in bonds and less in stocks to adjust its risk exposure for its aging investors.

Low-cost Funds—Unfortunately, professional money managers do not work for free. However, some mutual fund companies charge investors considerably lower fees and expenses than others. Some funds are sold only through a broker, and they will often—due to "loads" or sales commissions—cost considerably more than funds sold through a "no-load" mutual fund company. Vanguard is an example of a no-load mutual fund company where fees are very low. Many of their equity-oriented funds charge fees of 0.2% per year and under.

Money Manager—Also called "portfolio manager." The person (or sometimes a group) who manages your mutual fund.

Mutual Fund—A pooling of money from many investors by an investment company which then buys shares in various securities on behalf of its investors. Mutual funds invest in groups of securities in a single asset class (such as stocks, bonds, or real estate), or in a combination of several different asset classes. They may invest in domestic or foreign investments, or a combination of both. Mutual funds offer smaller investors the chance to gain professional management, diversification, and lower costs on small amounts of money.

No-load Funds—Mutual funds that do not charge investors sales commissions.

Pension Plan—Loosely, any investments directed toward providing income for a retiree during his or her retirement years. More precisely, it is a formal retirement plan provided by an employer for retirees in which the full cost of providing a monthly payment to the retiree is borne by the employer. Many companies that have had pension plans in the past are terminating them and substituting profit-sharing plans in their place.

Portfolio—The collection of stocks, bonds, cash, real estate (and so forth) that comprise an investor's holdings.

Profit-sharing Plan—A for-profit company's attempt to share its earnings with its employees and help them save for their retirements. See 401(k).

Prospectus—A legal document that describes how a mutual fund works. A valid prospectus must be sent to an investor before or at the same time he or she opens a new account.

Rebalancing—The act of realigning your investment allocation back to what it is supposed to be. Rebalancing should occur regularly (at least yearly) to make sure you are not overinvesting or underinvesting in the wrong assets.

Return—In investment lingo, it's how much you're making on your investments. Usually composed of increases (or decreases) in the market value of your underlying assets plus any dividends, distributions, or interest they may have paid.

Return Characteristics—A shorthand for the way assets behave, especially in relation to (or how they correlate with) other assets. Some rise when others rise; some fall when others rise. For instance, when stocks rise, bonds tend to fall. Good portfolios hold assets with a variety of return characteristics.

Roth IRA—An individual retirement arrangement (hence, "IRA") that allows an investor, during their working years, to contribute after-tax contributions to a personal retirement account and receive tax-free returns in retirement.

Roth 401(k) / 403(b)—A new, workplace retirement saving vehicle that allows employees to make after-tax payroll deduction contributions to their own workplace-based retirement savings plan. Different from 401(k) or 403(b) plans, in which contributions go into the plan untaxed and are then, in retirement, withdrawn as fully taxable, Roth 401(k) and Roth 403(b) contributions are taxed *before* they enter the employee's plan, and then, in retirement, are distributed to the employee tax free. Roth 401(k) and Roth 403(b) plans should be especially beneficial retirement savings plans for younger employees.

Stock—Also referred to as equity. Stock is an asset that shows ownership by its holder or investor and maintains a claim on the earnings and assets of an associated business.

Traditional IRA—An individual retirement arrangement (hence, "IRA") that allows a working person, during his or her working years, to make tax-deductible (or non-tax-deductible) contributions to a personal retirement account that will be permitted to grow untaxed until retirement. Then, in retirement, any withdrawals made by the employee will be fully taxed.

Volatility—The sometimes maddening up and down movements that are part of all investment markets.

APPENDIX
401(k) and 403(b) Plan Providers and Some Appropriate Mutual Funds They Offer

Below are listed the top 10 providers of retirement savings mutual funds to the 401(k) and the 403(b) markets.

401(k) plans are offered to employees of for-profit enterprises, while 403(b) plans serve the not-for-profit employee.

Leading 401(k) plan providers
(Assets listed are in millions, as of Dec. 31, 2006)

Manager	*Assets*
Fidelity Investments	$396,871
State Street Global	$172,221
Vanguard Group	$163,726
Capital Research	$105,895
T. Rowe Price	$70,676

Prudential Financial	$45,337
Principal Global Investors	$43,089
INVESCO	$39,245
Northern Trust Global Inv.	$36,026
JPMorgan Asset Mgmt.	$26,623

Leading 403(b) plan providers
(Assets listed are in millions, as of Dec. 31, 2006)

Manager	*Assets*
TIAA-CREF	$370,852
Fidelity Investments	$49,883
AIG Global Investments	$49,752
ING	$22,437
Capital Research	$15,807
Vanguard Group	$8,607
Prudential Financial	$7,694
MassMutual Financial	$6,344
American Century	$2,783
Federated Investors	$2,000

Asset Allocation Options

In most retirement savings programs, there is a wide array (too wide, in fact) of investment options to fulfill the diversification goals of your retirement savings plan.

Below, I have listed the specific funds for you to use, should your employer use any of the five large retirement plan providers listed. In some cases, you will still want to call the toll-free customer service phone numbers at those firms to get more specific information on your own account.

If your employer does not use one of the five fund groups listed below, call your retirement program's mutual fund toll-free investor service line (or speak to your human resources department first) and ask the mutual fund representative for a list of the most appropriate mutual funds for you to use that best satisfies the asset allocation goals among the six asset classes I have recommended to you in this book and that appear below.

Remember to keep in mind the specific type of fund you want and the overall percentage of your investments to be dedicated to each asset class in a well-diversified, equity-oriented portfolio, as described in the book:

> (U) US stocks – 35%
>
> (F) Developed foreign market stocks – 25%
>
> (E) Emerging foreign market stocks – 5%
>
> (R) Real estate – 15%
>
> (T) US Treasury bonds – 10%
>
> (I) Inflation-protected Treasuries – 10%

Remember to use low-cost index funds, wherever possible, to fill each asset category. Remember, too, that for the retirement saver who is NOT interested in selecting specific funds to fill out his or her allocation, many mutual fund retirement savings programs now offer lifecycle alternatives.

Some mutual fund providers may not have a fund, or one may not be available to you in your employer's plan, to fill each of the six asset allocation slots that you want filled. If that is the case, use the closest fund substitute available. Again, I would suggest that you talk to the fund company on their toll-free number and get suggestions that would best fit the asset categories I've laid out in the book.

Here are sample fund choices for five large 401(k) and 403(b) providers.

Fidelity Investment Funds

(U) Spartan US Equity Index Fund

(F) Spartan International Index Fund

(E) Fidelity Emerging Markets Fund

(R) Fidelity Real Estate Investment Portfolio

(T) Spartan Long-Term Treasury Bond Index

(I) Fidelity Inflation-Protected Bond Fund

TIAA-CREF

(U) CREF Equity Index

(F) International Equity Index

(E) No pure offering

(R) TIAA Real Estate

(T) No pure offering, try CREF Bond Market

(I) CREF Inflation-Linked

Vanguard*

(U) Total Stock Market Index

(F) Total International Stock Index

(E) Emerging Markets Stock Index

(R) REIT Index

(T) Long-Term Treasury Fund

(I) Inflation-Protected Securities Fund

Capital Research (American Funds)

(U) No pure offering, try The Growth Fund of America

(F) No pure offering, try New Perspective Fund

(E) No pure offering, try New World Fund

(R) No pure offering

(T) US Government Securities Fund

(I) No pure offering

State Street Global Advisors*

(U) SSgA S&P 500 Index Fund

(F) SSgA International Growth Opportunities Fund

(E) SSgA Emerging Markets Fund

(R) SSgA Tuckerman Active REIT Fund

(T) No pure offering, try SSgA Intermediate or Bond Market Fund

(I) No pure offering, try SSgA Intermediate or Bond Market Fund

Always remember you can call the toll-free investor service numbers at the mutual fund group that runs your company's plan to ask their service personnel to help you choose the funds that best satisfy the six asset allocations listed above (US stock, foreign markets, etc.). Ask for the best, lowest cost, diversified mix of ETFs, or ETFs and mutual funds.

* Both Vanguard and State Street Global Advisors offer a wide array of electronically-traded funds, or ETFs. ETFs, remember, are another form of mutual fund. If your plan allows for the use of ETFs with these providers, choose the ETF over the mutual funds.

ACKNOWLEDGMENTS

This book would never have seen the light of day, let alone been published, without the support and encouragement of Paul Santhouse, director of acquisitions for Moody Publishers. I thank Paul for his gentle persistence and friendship.

I also thank Chris Reese for his delicate touch in editing the final work, as well as extend my gratitude to a large group of others at Moody who work largely behind the scenes and on more projects at the same time than human beings can usually handle. But they somehow manage to do fine work.

Lastly, I thank my lovely bride of 37 years, Lizzie, whose own support, guidance, and patience with me on a project like this and lots else, too, demand the full measure of a woman's love.

ABOUT
THE AUTHOR

Jim O'Donnell was born in New York City and grew up in the Bronx. He graduated from Ivy League schools and for many years worked on Wall Street as a senior executive in the mutual fund business. In one year, he personally developed over $1.5 billion in new business. He has written for and spoken to national and international audiences on money and investments. In his mid-40s, he left the investment business to become a college professor at Huntington University, in Huntington, Indiana, where students later awarded him the honor of "Professor of the Year." Within months of arriving in Huntington, his wife Lizzie was diagnosed with terminal cancer. The fight to save Lizzie's life is the subject of Jim's first book, *Letters for Lizzie* (Northfield, 2004), which received front-page coverage in *The Wall*

Street Journal and led to a Pulitzer Prize for the author of the *Journal* article.

Jim's second book, *Walking with Arthur* (2005), a memoir praised by *The New York Times*, tells of Jim's spiritual journey. As a demanding, ambitious business-man, and before Lizzie's battle with cancer, Jim was in-creasingly disillusioned with the superficiality of the hard-driving world of Wall Street and found himself on the brink of divorce. In the midst of this chaos, he met a friend named Arthur and, through him, found God and an entirely new way of looking at life, family, and money.

WALKING WITH ARTHUR

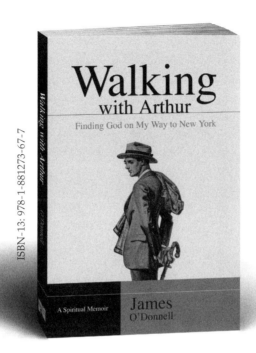

James O'Donnell's life was on the rocks. In one year, he experienced the
death of his father, a struggling marriage and a pay cut. His daily com-
mute partner, Arthur, never preached to him on their way to New York
City. They just walked . . . and God worked. Jim invites you to journey
alongside him, drawing you in with his gritty and honest candor.

 MOODY
PUBLISHERS.

1-800-678-8812 · MOODYPUBLISHERS.COM

LETTERS FOR LIZZIE

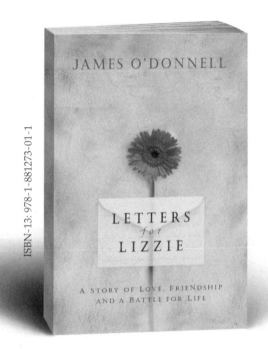

ISBN-13: 978-1-881273-01-1

James and Lizzie O'Donnell had everything. But they gave up the money, lovely homes and nearby friends and family to move to a small town and serve others. Within three months, Lizzie was diagnosed with terminal cancer. *Letters for Lizzie* is a remarkable true story of a husband's love for his sick wife.

1-800-678-8812 · MOODYPUBLISHERS.COM